HARRAP'S

Japanese phrasebook

Tessa Carroll
Harumi Currie

McGraw-Hill

New York Chicago San Francisco Lisbon London Madrid Mexico City
Milan New Delhi San Juan Seoul Singapore Sydney Toronto

ISBN 0-07-148249-0

McGraw-Hill books are available at special quantity discounts to use as
premiums and sales promotions, or for use in corporate training programs.
For more information, please write to the Director of Special Sales,
Professional Publishing, McGraw-Hill, Two Penn Plaza, New York, NY
10121-2298. Or contact your local bookstore.

Editor & Project Manager
Anna Stevenson

Publishing Manager
Patrick White

Prepress
Heather Macpherson

CONTENTS

CONTENTS

INTRODUCTION

This brand new English-Japanese phrasebook from Harrap is ideal for anyone wishing to try out their foreign language skills while travelling abroad. The information is practical and clearly presented, helping you to overcome the language barrier and mix with the locals.

Each section features a list of useful words and a selection of common phrases: some of these you will read or hear, while others will help you to express yourself. The simple phonetic transcription system, specifically designed for English speakers, ensures that you will always make yourself understood.

The book also includes a mini bilingual dictionary of some 2,200 words, so that more adventurous users can build on the basic structures and engage in more complex conversations.

Concise information on local culture and customs is provided, along with practical tips to save you time. After all, you're on holiday – time to relax and enjoy yourself! There is also a food and drink glossary to help you make sense of menus, and ensure that you don't miss out on any of the national or regional specialities.

Remember that any effort you make will be appreciated. So don't be shy – have a go!

ABBREVIATIONS USED IN THIS BOOK

adj	adjective
adv	adverb
n	noun
prep	preposition
v	verb
vi	intransitive verb
vt	transitive verb

PRONUNCIATION

The range of sounds in Japanese is smaller than in English, and pronunciation presents no great difficulties for English speakers, as long as some key points are noted.

Japanese syllables consist of one of the following:

1. a vowel alone (eg *a*)
2. a consonant followed by a vowel (eg *ka*)
3. *n*, which counts as a syllable in its own right
4. a consonant followed by *y* followed by a vowel (eg *kya*).

Each syllable is pronounced as one "beat" and there is no stress on a particular syllable within a word; this is an important difference from English.

Each vowel has one particular sound that does not change. When different vowels follow each other, each is clearly pronounced; for example, *aoi* (blue) is pronounced *a-o-i*. Nor do the vowel sounds change when combined with different consonants; for example, *kane* (money) is pronounced *ka-ne*.

Here are the syllables of Japanese, presented in traditional Japanese order, with a guide to their pronunciation:

Vowels

a   as in "c**a**r" but shorter

i   as in "f**ee**t" but shorter

u   as in "b**oo**k", but shorter and with lips less rounded

e   as in "b**e**d"

o   as in "h**o**t" but with lips slightly more rounded

Consonants followed by vowels

The consonants are similar to English ones, apart from where noted:

ka, ki, ku, ke, ko

ga, gi, gu, ge, go (g is sometimes nasalized, like the "ng" in "si**ng**", particularly in the Tokyo area, but it is not necessary to do so)

sa, shi, su, se, so

za, ji, zu, ze, zo

ta, chi, tsu (as in "ba**ts**"), *te, to*

da, ji, zu, de, do

na, ni, nu, ne, no

ha, hi, fu (pronounced without the upper teeth touching the lower lip, so between the English sounds "f" and "h"), *he, ho*

pa, pi, pu, pe, po

ba, bi, bu, be, bo

ma, mi, mu, me, mo

ya, yu, yo

ra, ri, ru, re, ro (the r sound is between the English sounds "r" and "l")

wa (with lips less rounded than for the English sound "w")

n (pronounced and written here as *m* before *p*, *b* and *m*; for example *kampai* cheers!; *shimbun* newspaper; *sam bamme* third, and as nasal *n*, like the "n" in "si**ng**" before all other sounds or at the end of words, for example *onsen* hot spring. This is written as *n'* before vowels and *y*, for example *kin'en* non-smoking, compared with *kinen* (*ki-nen*) commemoration.

If *i* or *u* occurs between any of the consonants *k*, *s*, *t*, *h* and *p*, they are usually whispered so they are barely heard; for example, the name *Yamashita* sounds like *Yamashta*. This also happens at the end of words, particularly verbs ending in *su*; for example, *ikimasu* (go) is often pronounced *ikimas*.

Each of the vowels can be lengthened, so that the syllable lasts for two beats. This is shown by a circumflex over the vowel: *â, î, û, ê, ô*. The vowel sounds are the same as described above – just hold the sound of a long vowel for twice as long. It is important to distinguish between short and long vowels, as some words are identical apart from this difference; for example *shujin* (husband, host) and *shûjin* (prisoner). Here are some more examples of short and long vowels: *futsû* (ordinary, normal – short vowel then long vowel), *fûfu* (married couple – long vowel then short vowel), *kinô* (yesterday – short vowel then long vowel).

The consonants *k, s, t* and p can also be lengthened; again, it is important to pronounce double consonants with two beats. For example, *kk* in *gakkô* is pronounced as in "bla**ck c**at". Note that when *ch* is doubled, it is written as *tch*. Similarly, when *n* is followed by *na, ni, ne, ne* or *no*, the *n* is pronounced as well as the syllable that follows; for example *kinnen (kin-nen)* – recent years, compared to *kinen (ki-nen)* – commemoration.

Writing system

The Japanese writing system combines Chinese characters (*kanji*), which convey an element of meaning (concept or object) as well as sound, and two phonetic syllabaries, (*hiragana* and *katakana*. Each syllable can be written using two different types of character, *hiragana* and *katakana*. Any Japanese words can be written in *hiragana*, but this script is mainly used to write grammatical words and endings of words where the main part that conveys the concept is written in *kanji*. The *katakana* script is used mainly for loanwords of foreign origin. Japanese was traditionally written vertically, right to left, but is now also written horizontally, left to right, and there are no breaks between words.

EVERYDAY CONVERSATION

You should respect the basic rules of Japanese etiquette, which include taking your shoes off when you enter someone's house, not leaving your chopsticks sticking up in the rice, not eating while walking about and blowing your nose discreetly if you can't avoid doing so. It is also considered good manners to give **omiyage**, or small gifts, when visiting people, attending ceremonies or returning from your travels.

The Japanese speak quite formally to each other – more familiar language is only used with close friends and family, or by young people who are part of the same group of friends. It is considered rude to reply with a flat refusal or an overly strong opinion. Euphemisms are often used to express negative opinions, but be careful as they can be misunderstood. You should also bear in mind that the Japanese consider it childish to make excuses – the expression *môshiwake gozaimasen* literally means "I have no excuse".

Greetings are formal, with no kissing or hugging. Among friends, a slight nod of the head is acceptable, but more obvious bowing is needed in a more formal environment, say when meeting older people or new work acquaintances. The lower the bow and the longer it lasts, the greater the formality. You should bow from the waist, keeping your neck and back straight from head to hips. Women should place one hand over the other with their arms held down in front of their bodies, and men should keep their arms at their sides. You should also try to avoid too much direct eye contact.

Many gestures are different in Japan. For example, to beckon someone towards you, move your fingers in your usual gesture but with your palm facing downwards. When pointing to yourself, point towards the tip of your nose with your index finger.

EVERYDAY CONVERSATION

The basics

bye	バイバイ *bai bai*
excuse me	すみません *sumimasen*
goodbye	さようなら *sayônara*
good evening	こんばんは *kombanwa*
good morning	おはようございます *ohayô gozaimasu* (only used until around 10am; after that, use こんにちは *konnichiwa*)
goodnight	おやすみなさい *oyasumi nasai*
hello	こんにちは *konnichiwa*
no	いいえ *îe*
OK	オッケー *okkê*
pardon *(excuse me)*	すみません *sumimasen*
pardon?	何ですか *nan desu ka?*
please	お願いします *onegai shimasu*
thanks, thank you	ありがとう（ございます）*arigatô (gozaimasu)*
yes	はい *hai*, ええ *ê*

Expressing yourself

I'd/we'd like …
… をください。
… o kudasai

do you want …?
… がほしいですか。
… ga hoshî desu ka?

do you have …?
… はありますか。
… wa arimasu ka?

is there a …?/are there any …?
… はありますか。
… wa arimasu ka?

how?
どう
dô?

why?
なぜ・どうして
naze/dôshite?

when?
いつ
itsu?

what?
なに・なん
nani/nan?

where is/are ...?
... はどこですか。
... wa doko desu ka?

how much is it?
いくらですか。
ikura desu ka?

what is it?
何ですか。
nan desu ka?

do you speak English?
英語が話せますか。
êgo ga hanasemasu ka?

where are the toilets, please?
すみません、トイレはどこですか。
sumimasen, toire wa doko desu ka?

how are you?
お元気ですか。
ogenki desu ka?

fine, thanks
ええ、元気です。
ê, genki desu

thanks very much
どうもありがとうございます。
dômo arigatô gozaimasu

no, thanks
いいえ、結構です。
îe, kekkô desu

yes, please
はい、お願いします。
hai, onegai shimasu

you're welcome
どういたしまして。
dô itashimashite

see you later
では、また。
dewa, mata

I'm sorry
すみません。
sumimasen

Understanding

注意 *chûi*	attention
... 禁止 ... *kinshi*	do not ...
入口 *iriguchi*	entrance
出口 *deguchi*	exit
無料 *muryô*	free
駐車禁止 *chûsha kinshi*	no parking
禁煙 *kin'en*	no smoking
オープン *ôpun*, 営業中 *êgyô chû*	open

故障中 *koshô chû*	out of order
予約席 *yoyaku seki*	reserved
お手洗い *otearai,*	toilets
トイレ *toire*	

... があります。
... ga arimasu
there's/there are ... *(for things)*

... がいます。
... ga imasu
there's/there are ... *(for people and animals)*

いらっしゃいませ。
irasshaimase
welcome

...てもいいですか。
... te mo î desu ka?
do you mind if ...?

ちょっと、お待ちください。
chotto omachi kudasai
one moment, please

おかけください・お座りください。
okake kudasai/osuwari kudasai
please take a seat

PROBLEMS UNDERSTANDING JAPANESE

Expressing yourself

pardon?
何ですか。
nan desu ka?

what?
何ですか。
nan desu ka?

could you speak more slowly?
もう少しゆっくり話してください。
mô sukoshi yukkuri hanashite kudasai

I don't understand
わかりません。
wakarimasen

I understand a little Japanese
日本語は少ししか分かりません。
nihongo wa sukoshi shika wakarimasen

I can understand Japanese but I can't speak it
日本語は分かりますが、話せません。
nihongo wa wakarimasu ga, hanasemasen

I hardly speak any Japanese
日本語はほとんど話せません。
nihongo wa hotondo hanasemasen

do you speak English?
英語は話せますか。
êgo wa hanasemasu ka?

how do you say ... in Japanese?
... は日本語で何と言いますか。
... wa nihongo de nan to îmasu ka?

what's that called in Japanese?
日本語では何と呼びますか。
nihongo de wa nan to yobimasu ka?

could you write it down for me?
書いてもらえますか。
kaite moraemasu ka?

Understanding

日本語は分かりますか。
nihongo wa wakarimasu ka?
do you understand Japanese?

書いてあげましょう。
kaite agemashô
I'll write it down for you

それは ... という意味です。
sore wa ... to yû imi desu
it means ...

それは … のようなものです。
sore wa … no yô na mono desu
it's a kind of …

どういうつづりですか。
dô yû tsuzuri desu ka?
how do you spell it?

SPEAKING ABOUT THE LANGUAGE

Expressing yourself

I learned a few words from my phrasebook
海外旅行者用の本で、少しだけ覚えました。
kaigai ryokôsha yô no hon de sukoshi dake oboemashita

I can just about get by
何とか分かります。
nantoka wakarimasu

I hardly know two words!
全く分かりません。
mattaku wakarimasen

I find Japanese a difficult language
日本語は難しい言葉だと思います。
nihongo wa muzukashî kotoba da to omoimasu

I know the basics but no more than that
基本的なことしか分かりません。
kihonteki na koto shika wakarimasen

people speak too quickly for me
みんな話し方が早すぎます。
minna hanashikata ga hayasugimasu

Understanding

発音がいいですね。
hatsuon ga î desu ne
you have a good accent

日本語がとてもじょうずですね。
nihongo ga totemo jôzu desu ne
you speak very good Japanese

ASKING THE WAY

Expressing yourself

excuse me, can you tell me where the … is, please?
すみません、… はどこか教えてください。
sumimasen, … wa doko ka oshiete kudasai

which way is it to …?
… へ行く道はどちらですか。
… e iku michi wa dochira desu ka?

can you tell me how to get to …?
… へどうやって行くか教えてもらえませんか。
… e dô yatte iku ka oshiete moraemasen ka?

is there a … near here?
この近くに … がありますか。
kono chikaku ni … ga arimasu ka?

could you show me on the map?
この地図で教えてくれませんか。
kono chizu de oshiete kuremasen ka?

is there a map of the town somewhere?
どこかにこの町の地図はありますか。
doko ka ni kono machi no chizu wa arimasu ka?

is it far?
遠いですか。
tôi desu ka?

I'm looking for …
… を探しています。
… o sagashite imasu

I'm lost
道に迷いました。
michi ni mayoimashita

Understanding

に沿っていく *ni sotte iku*	follow
降りる *oriru*, 下る *kudaru*	go down
上る *noboru*, 上がる *agaru*	go up
そのまま行く *sono mama iku*	keep going
左 *hidari*	left
右 *migi*	right
まっすぐ *massugu*	straight ahead
曲がる *magaru*	to turn

歩いて行きますか。
aruite ikimasu ka?
are you on foot?

車で5分です。
kuruma de go fun desu
it's five minutes away by car

最初・2番目・3番目の角を左です。
saisho/nibamme/sambamme no kado o hidari desu
it's the first/second/third turning on the left

左側の最初・2番目・3番目の ... です。
hidari gawa no saisho/nibamme/sambamme no ... desu
it's the first/second/third ... on the left

交差点を右に曲がってください。
kôsaten o migi ni magatte kudasai
turn right at the crossroads

銀行を左に曲がってください。
ginkô o hidari ni magatte kudasai
turn left at the bank

次の出口で出てください。
tsugi no deguchi de dete kudasai
take the next exit

そんなに遠くありません。
sonna ni tôku arimasen
it's not far

すぐそこです。
sugu soko desu
it's just round the corner

Japanese has different registers of language depending on formality and the degree of closeness between the people involved. These can broadly be described as affectionate, friendly familiar, friendly polite, polite and very polite.

Within the family, affectionate terms of address are used: dad (**otôsan**), mum (**okâsan**), big sister (**onêsan**) and big brother (**onîsan**). The **san** suffix (or title) is only used for older family members, and younger brothers and sisters are referred to by their given names, often with the suffix **chan** added, for example, Mika-chan. Note that **chan** can also be used for older family members (eg **onêchan**) and close friends, who may also have nicknames. Boys and young men are also addressed with the familiar title **kun** after their names.

The friendly familiar register is used among young people of the same age (classmates etc) and within the family.

The friendly polite register (used in this guide) and the polite register are used when speaking to friends, acquaintances, neighbours and fellow students of different ages (this is known as the **sempai/kôhai** or younger/ older relationship). The suffix **san** is added after the first name or family name. Family names come before first names in Japanese. Note that direct use of pronouns meaning "you" is considered rude and aggressive, and names with titles are used instead.

The extremely polite register (**kêgo**) is used when speaking to strangers and distant acquaintances, and by shop assistants, hotel and transport staff, and others dealing with customers.

The basics

bad	よくない *yokunai*, 悪い *warui*
beautiful	きれい *kirê*
boring	つまらない *tsumaranai*
cheap	安い *yasui*
cute	かわいい *kawaî*
expensive	高い *takai*
good	いい *î*
great	すごい *sugoi*
interesting	面白い *omoshiroi*
nice	すてき *suteki*
not bad	悪くない *warukunai*
pretty	かわいい *kawaî*
well	よく *yoku*
to hate	嫌い *kirai*
to like	好き *suki*
to love	大好き *dai suki*

INTRODUCING YOURSELF AND FINDING OUT ABOUT OTHER PEOPLE

Expressing yourself

my name's ...
私の名前は ... です。
watashi no namae wa ... desu

what's your name?
お名前は。
onamae wa?

how do you do!
初めまして。
hajimemashite

pleased to meet you!
どうぞ、よろしく。
dôzo yoroshiku

this is my husband/wife
主人・家内です。
shujin/kanai desu

this is my partner, Karen
パートナーのカレンです。
pâtonâ no karen desu

I'm/we're English/Welsh/Scottish/Irish/British
イングランド人・ウェールズ人・スコットランド人・アイルランド人
・イギリス人です。
ingurandojin/wêruzujin/sukottorandojin/airurandojin/igirisujin desu

I'm from ...
... から来ました。
... kara kimashita

where are you from?
出身はどこですか。
shusshin wa doko desu ka?

how old are you?
おいくつですか。
oikutsu desu ka?

I'm 22
22歳です。
nijûni sai desu

what do you do for a living?
お仕事は何ですか。
oshigoto wa nan desu ka?

are you a student?
学生ですか。
gakusê desu ka?

I work
働いています。
hataraite imasu

I'm studying law
法律を勉強しています。
hôritsu o benkyô shite imasu

I'm a teacher
教師です。
kyôshi desu

I stay at home with the children
家で子供の面倒を見ています。
ie de kodomo no mendô o mite imasu

I work part-time
パートタイムで働いています。
pâto taimu de hataraite imasu

I work in marketing
マーケティングをしています。
mâketingu o shite imasu

I'm retired
退職しました。
taishoku shimashita

I'm self-employed
自営業です。
jiêgyô desu

I have two children
子供が二人います。
kodomo ga futari imasu

we don't have any children
子供はいません。
kodomo wa imasen

two boys and a girl
息子が二人と娘が一人。
musuko ga futari to museme ga hitori

a boy of five and a girl of two
５歳の息子と２歳の娘。
go sai no musuko to ni sai no musume

have you ever been to Britain?
イギリスに行ったことがありますか。
igirisu ni itta koto ga arimasu ka?

GETTING TO
KNOW PEOPLE

Understanding

イングランド人ですか。
ingurandojin desu ka?
are you English?

イングランドのことをよく知っています。
ingurando no koto o yoku shitte imasu
I know England quite well

私たちも休暇です。
watashi-tachi mo kyûka desu
we're on holiday here too

いつかスコットランドに行ってみたいです。
itsuka sukottorando ni itte mitai desu
I'd love to go to Scotland one day

TALKING ABOUT YOUR STAY

Expressing yourself

I'm here on business
仕事で来ました。
shigoto de kimashita

we're on holiday
休暇で来ました。
kyûka de kimashita

I arrived three days ago
３日前に来ました。
mikka mae ni kimashita

we've been here for a week
一週間、ここにいます。
isshûkan koko ni imasu

this is our first time in Japan
初めて日本に来ました。
hajimete nihon ni kimashita

we're just passing through
ちょっと立ち寄っただけです。
chotto tachiyotta dake desu

I'm only here for a long weekend
ここには週末だけです。
koko ni wa shûmatsu dake desu

we're here to celebrate our wedding anniversary
結婚記念のお祝いで来ました。
kekkon kinen no oiwai de kimashita

GETTING TO
KNOW PEOPLE

19

we're on our honeymoon
新婚旅行中です。
shinkon ryokô chû desu

we're touring around
周遊旅行で来ています。
shûyû ryokô de kite imasu

we're here with friends
友達と来ています。
tomodachi to kite imasu

we managed to get a cheap flight
安い航空券が手に入りました。
yasui kôkûken ga te ni hairimashita

Understanding

よい旅行を。
yoi ryokô o
have a good trip!

どのぐらいいますか。
dono gurai imasu ka?
how long are you staying?

… には行かれましたか。
… ni wa ikaremashita ka?
have you been to …?

日本は初めてですか。
nihon wa hajimete desu ka?
is this your first time in Japan?

ここはお気に召しましたか。
koko wa oki ni meshimashita ka?
do you like it here?

STAYING IN TOUCH

Expressing yourself

we should stay in touch
これからも連絡ください。
kore kara mo renraku kudasai

I'll give you my e-mail address
私のメールアドレスを教えましょう。
watashi no mêru adoresu o oshiemashô

here's my address, if ever you come to Britain
もしイギリスに来ることがあれば、これが私の住所です。
moshi igirisu ni kuru koto ga areba, kore ga watashi no jûsho desu

Understanding

住所を教えてくださいますか。
jûsho o oshiete kudasaimasu ka?
will you give me your address?

メールアドレスはありますか。
mêru adoresu wa arimasu ka?
do you have an e-mail address?

いつでもうちに来て泊まってください。
itsudemo uchi ni kite tomatte kudasai
you're always welcome to come and stay with us here

EXPRESSING YOUR OPINION

It is considered rude to express open disagreement, unless you clearly have higher status than the other person, so the Japanese tend to use vaguer phrases whose meanings are nevertheless understood by both sides.

Expressing yourself

I really like ...
... がとても好きです。
... ga totemo suki desu

I really liked ...
... がとても好きでした。
... ga totemo suki deshita

I don't like ...
... は好きじゃありません。
... wa suki ja arimasen

I didn't like ...
... は好きじゃありませんでした。
... wa suki ja arimasen deshita

I love ...
... 大好きです。
... dai suki desu

I loved ...
... 大好きでした。
... dai suki deshita

I would like to ...
... たいです。
... tai desu (see grammar)

I would have liked to ...
... たかったです。
... takatta desu (see grammar)

GETTING TO
KNOW PEOPLE

21

I find it ...
... と思います。
... to omoimasu

it's lovely
すばらしい。
subarashî

I agree
私もそう思います。
watashi mo sô omoimasu

I don't know
わかりません。
wakarimasen

I don't like the sound of ...
ううん、ちょっと … 。
ûn, chotto ...

it really annoys me
困りました。
komarimashita

it's a rip-off
ぼったくりだ。
bottakuri da

it's too busy
すごく混んでいます。
sugoku konde imasu

I/we had a great time
とても楽しかったです。
totemo tanoshikatta desu

I'm tired
疲れました。
tsukaremashita

there was a really good atmosphere
とてもいい雰囲気でした。
totemo î fun'iki deshita

I found it ...
... と思いました。
... to omoimashita

it was lovely
すばらしかったです。
subarashikatta desu

I don't agree
そうですか、私はちょっと。
sô desu ka. watashi wa chotto

I don't mind
かまいませんよ。
kamaimasen yo

it sounds interesting
面白そうですね。
omoshirosô desu ne

it was boring
つまらなかったです。
tsumaranakatta desu

it gets very busy at night
夜はとても混みます。
yoru wa totemo komimasu

it's very quiet
とても静かです。
totemo shizuka desu

we met some nice people
いい人達と出会いました。
î hito-tachi to deaimashita

we found a great hotel
すばらしいホテルを見つけました。
subarashî hoteru o mitsukemashita

Understanding

… は好きですか。
… wa suki desu ka?
do you like …?

楽しかったですか。
tanoshikatta desu ka?
did you enjoy yourselves?

… へ行った方がいいですよ。
… e itta hô ga î desu yo
you should go to …

… をお勧めします。
… o osusume shimasu
I recommend …

素敵な所です。
suteki na tokoro desu
it's a lovely area

観光客はあまりいません。
kankô kyaku wa amari imasen
there aren't too many tourists

週末は行かないほうがいいです。とても混んでいます。
shûmatsu wa ikanai hô ga î desu. totemo konde imasu
don't go at the weekend, it's too busy

評判ほどではないです。
hyôban hodo de wa nai desu
it's a bit overrated

TALKING ABOUT THE WEATHER

Expressing yourself

have you seen the weather forecast for tomorrow?
明日の天気予報を見ましたか。
ashita no tenki yohô o mimashita ka?

it's going to be nice
晴れるでしょう。
hareru deshô

it isn't going to be nice
天気はあまりよくないでしょう。
tenki wa amari yokunai deshô

it's really hot/cold
とても暑い・寒いです。
totemo atsui/samui desu

it gets cold at night
夜は冷え込みます。
yoru wa hiekomimasu

the weather was beautiful
天気はすばらしかったです。
tenki wa subarashikatta desu

it rained a few times
何回か雨が降りました。
nan kai ka ame ga furimashita

there was a thunderstorm
すごい雷でした。
sugoi kaminari deshita

it's been lovely all week
一週間ずっといい天気でした。
isshûkan zutto î tenki deshita

it's very humid here
ここはとても蒸します。
koko wa totemo mushimasu

we've been lucky with the weather
天気には恵まれていました。
tenki ni wa megumarete imashita

it's hot and sticky, isn't it?
蒸し暑いですね。
mushiatsui desu ne

it's raining a lot, isn't it?
よく降りますね。
yoku furimasu ne

Understanding

雨が降るそうです。
ame ga furu sô desu
it's supposed to rain

梅雨です。
tsuyu desu
it's the rainy season

今週末まで天気がいいそうです。
kon shûmatsu made tenki ga î sô desu
they've forecast good weather for the rest of the week

明日も暑いでしょう。
ashita mo atsui deshô
it will be hot again tomorrow

 GETTING TO KNOW PEOPLE

 24

TRAVELLING

The basics

airport	空港 *kûkô*
boarding	搭乗 *tôjô*
boarding card	搭乗券 *tôjôken*
boat	船 *fune*
booking	予約 *yoyaku*
bullet train	新幹線 *shinkansen*
bus	バス *basu*
bus station	バスターミナル *basu tâminaru*
bus stop	バス停 *basu tê*
car	車 *kuruma*, 自動車 *jidôsha*
check-in	チェックイン *chekkuin*
coach	長距離バス *chôkyori basu*
ferry	フェリー *ferî*
flight	便 *bin*
gate	ゲート *gêto*
left-luggage lockers	コインロッカー *koin rokkâ*
left-luggage (office)	手荷物預かり所 *tenimotsu azukarijo*
luggage	荷物 *nimotsu*
map	地図 *chizu*
motorway	高速道路 *kôsoku dôro*
passport	パスポート *pasupôto*
plane	飛行機 *hikôki*
platform	(プラット) ホーム *(puratto)hômu*
railway station	駅 *eki*
return (ticket)	往復 (切符) *ôfuku (kippu)*
road	道路 *dôro*
shuttle bus	シャトルバス *shatoru basu*
single (ticket)	片道 (切符) *katamichi (kippu)*
street	通り *tôri*
streetmap	ストリートマップ *sutorîto mappu*
taxi	タクシー *takushî*
terminal	ターミナル *tâminaru*
ticket	チケット *chiketto*, 切符 *kippu*
timetable	時刻表 *jikokuhyô*

TRAVELLING

tourist bus	観光バス *kankô basu*
town centre	中心街 *chûshingai*
train	列車 *ressha*, 電車 *densha*
tram	路面電車 *romen densha*, 市電 *shiden*
underground	地下鉄 *chikatetsu*
underground station	地下鉄の駅 *chikatetsu no eki*
to book	予約する *yoyaku suru*
to hire	借りる *kariru*

Expressing yourself

where can I buy tickets?
切符はどこで買ったらいいですか。
kippu wa doko de kattara î desu ka?

a ticket to ..., please
… までの切符をお願いします。
... made no kippu o onegai shimasu

I'd like to book a ticket
切符を予約したいんですが。
kippu o yoyaku shitai n desu ga

how much is a ticket to ...?
… までの切符はいくらですか。
... made no kippu wa ikura desu ka?

are there any concessions for students?
学割はききますか。
gakuwari wa kikimasu ka?

could I have a timetable, please?
時刻表をください。
jikokuhyô o kudasai

is there an earlier/later one?
それより早い・遅いのはありますか。
sore yori hayai/osoi no wa arimasu ka?

how long does the journey take?
どのくらい時間がかかりますか。
dono kurai jikan ga kakarimasu ka?

is this seat free?
ここは空いていますか。
koko wa aite imasu ka?

I'm sorry, there's someone sitting there
すみません。ここは人が来ます。
sumimasen. koko wa hito ga kimasu

Understanding

到着 *tôchaku*	arrivals
キャンセル *kyanseru*, 中止 *chûshi*	cancelled
乗り換え *norikae*	connections
出発 *shuppatsu*	departures
入口 *iriguchi*	entrance
立入禁止 *tachi-hiri kinshi*	no entry
案内 *annai*	information
遅延 *chien*	delayed
出口 *deguchi*	exit
男性用トイレ *dansê yô toire*	gents
女性用トイレ *josê yô toire*	ladies
切符 *kippu*, チケット *chiketto*	tickets
お手洗い *otearai*, トイレ *toire*	toilets

満員です。
man'in desu
everything is fully booked

BY PLANE

It can sometimes work out cheaper to take domestic flights than the high-speed "bullet trains" (新幹線 *shinkansen*). By booking a few months in advance you can find some good discounts, particularly on early-morning flights. The main travel agencies in Japan are HIS and JTB.

Expressing yourself

where's the British Airways check-in?
英国航空 ブリティッシュエアウェイ のチェックインはどこですか。
êkoku kôkû buritisshu eawê no chekkuin wa doko desu ka?

I've got an e-ticket
イーチケットを持っています。
î-chiketto o motte imasu

what time do we board?
搭乗は何時ですか。
tôjô wa nanji desu ka?

one suitcase and one piece of hand luggage
スーツケースがひとつと手荷物がひとつです。
sûtsukêsu ga hitotsu to tenimotsu ga hitotsu desu

I'd like to confirm my return flight
帰りの飛行機のリコンファームをしたいんですが。
kaeri no hikôki no rikonfâmu o shitai n desu ga

one of my suitcases is missing
スーツケースがひとつ足りません。
sûtsukêsu ga hitotsu tarimasen

my luggage hasn't arrived
荷物がまだ来ていません。
nimotsu ga mada kite imasen

the plane was two hours late
飛行機が２時間遅れました。
hikôki ga ni jikan okuremashita

I've missed my connection
乗り換え損ねました。
norikae sokonemashita

I've left something on the plane
飛行機の中に忘れ物をしました。
hikôki no naka ni wasuremono o shimashita

I want to report the loss of my luggage
着いていない荷物の届け出をしたいんですが。
tsuite inai nimotsu no todokede o shitai n desu ga

Understanding

荷物受取所 *nimotsu uketorijo*	baggage reclaim
チェックイン *chekkuin*	check-in
税関 *zêkan*	customs
出発ロビー *shuppatsu robî*	departure lounge

国内線 *kokunai sen*	domestic flights
免税 *menzê*	duty free
申告が必要なもの *shinkoku ga hitsuyô na mono*	goods to declare
すぐに搭乗 *sugu ni tôjô*	immediate boarding
申告するものがない *shinkoku suru mono ga nai*	nothing to declare
入国審査 *nyûkoku shinsa*	passport control

出発ロビーでお待ちください。
shuppatsu robî de omachi kudasai
please wait in the departure lounge

窓側と通路側とどちらのお席がよろしいですか。
madogawa to tsûrogawa to dochira no oseki ga yoroshî desu ka?
would you like a window seat or an aisle seat?

… でお乗換えください。
… de onorikae kudasai
you'll have to change in …

お荷物はおいくつですか。
onimotsu wa oikutsu desu ka?
how many bags do you have?

ご自分でお荷物はお詰めになりましたか。
gojibun de onimotsu wa otsume ni narimashita ka?
did you pack all your bags yourself?

人から持って行ってくれと頼まれたものはありませんか。
hito kara motte itte kure to tanomareta mono wa arimasen ka?
has anyone given you anything to take on board?

お荷物は5キロ、制限重量をオーバーしております。
onimotsu wa go kiro seigen jûryô o ôbâ shite orimasu
your luggage is five kilos overweight

搭乗券をどうぞ。
tôjôken o dôzo
here's your boarding card

搭乗は … 時から始まります。
tôjô wa … ji kara hajimarimasu
boarding will begin at …

… 番ゲートにお進みください。
… ban gêto ni osusumi kudasai
please proceed to gate number …

… 様、最後のお呼び出しでございます。
… sama, saigo no oyobidashi de gozaimasu
this is a final call for …

お荷物が到着したかどうかは、この電話番号でご確認ください。
*onimotsu ga tôchaku shita ka dô ka wa, kono denwa bangô de gokakunin
  kudasai*
you can call this number to check if your luggage has arrived

BY TRAIN, COACH, BUS, UNDERGROUND, TRAM

The Japanese rail network is dense, and concentrated around the Pacific coast cities. The bullet train (新幹線 *shinkansen*) links the main cities, while the privatized rail company Japanese Railway (JR) serves the thousands of small local stations all over the country. There are also many local private rail companies. A Japan Railpass, valid for 7, 14 or 21 days, allows standard-class travel on the whole JR network, including all but the fastest bullet trains, and can be very good value. See http://www.japanrailpass.net/eng/en00.html

Train fares are calculated according to distance and type of train: super express (特急 *tokkyû*), express (急行 *kyûkô*), semi-express (準急 *junkyû*) or slow (普通 *futsû*).

Carriages are divided into first class (グリーン車 *gurîn sha*), second class with reservation (指定席 *shitê seki*) and second class without reservation (自由席 *jiyû seki*).

Trains generally run on time, barring natural disasters (typhoons, hurricanes and snowstorms are not uncommon in some areas).

In the cities commuter trains are extremely crowded at peak times. Whatever company you travel with, there are machines at most station exits to adjust automatically the price of your ticket if you have travelled further than you originally intended. If you're not sure where you're going or can't read the price for a destination written in Japanese, you can just buy the cheapest ticket and pay the excess when you arrive. You will never be suspected of trying to cheat if there is an on-train ticket inspection.

During the Japanese school holidays in spring, summer and winter, the JR company offers a very good value ticket called the 青春十八切符 *seishun jûhachi kippu*. Although this means "under 18s ticket", there is in fact no age limit. It allows you to make any journey on JR's local lines in a 24-hour period. The longer the journey, the more changes you will have to make: it can take at least eight hours to get from Tokyo to Kyoto. Unused tickets are refundable.

For the underground and local trains, you can get monthly passes (定期 *têki*) to save you having to queue up at the automatic ticket machines. The network is not divided into zones – a *têki* is valid from one point to another, on a designated rail line. When you change from one private line to another, you usually have to pay twice, although companies do have agreements which reduce the cost slightly if you buy a ticket for the whole journey before you set off.

Buses are not only for travel within cities but can be used over long distances too. The overnight buses are affordable and reasonably comfortable (from Tokyo to Kyoto takes about six hours). You can buy tickets when you get on or off the bus. Press the button to request a stop.

Train timetables are drawn up in the same way as ours, in table form with the times running vertically. There is a special red timetable for Sundays and holidays.

Expressing yourself

can I have a map of the underground, please?
地下鉄の路線図をください。
chikatetsu no rosenzu o kudasai

what time is the next train to ...?
... 行きの次の列車は何時ですか。
... yuki no tsugi no ressha wa nan ji desu ka?

what time is the last train?
最終列車は何時ですか。
saishû ressha wa nan ji desu ka?

which platform is it for …?
… 行きは何番ホーム /何番線 からですか。
… yuki wa namban hômu/namban sen kara desu ka?

where can I catch a bus to …?
… 行きのバスはどこですか。
… yuki no basu wa doko desu ka?

which line do I take to get to …?
… に行くのにはどの線に乗ればいいですか。
… ni iku no ni wa dono sen ni noreba î desu ka?

is this the bus stop for …?
… 行きのバス停はここですか。
… yuki no basu tê wa koko desu ka?

is this where the coach leaves for …?
ここから … 行きのバスが出ますか。
koko kara … yuki no basu ga demasu ka?

can you tell me when I need to get off?
私が降りる所に来たら、教えてくれませんか。
watashi ga oriru tokoro ni kitara, oshiete kuremasen ka?

I've missed my train/bus
列車・バスに乗り遅れました。
ressha/basu ni noriokuremashita

Understanding

改札口 *kaisatsuguchi*	ticket barrier
切符売り場 *kippu uriba*	ticket office
本日出発分 *honjitsu shuppatsu bun*	tickets for travel today
週ごとの *shûgoto no*	weekly
一ヶ月毎の *ikkagetsugoto no*	monthly
本日の *honjitsu no*	for the day
予約 *yoyaku*	bookings
大人 *otona*	adult
小人 *kodomo*	child

右にもう少し行った所にバス停があります。
migi ni mô sukoshi itta tokoro ni basu tê ga arimasu
there's a stop a bit further along on the right

お釣りがないようにお願いします。
otsuri ga nai yô ni onegai shimasu
exact money only, please

… で乗り換えてください。
… de norikaete kudasai
you'll have to change at …

… 番のバスにお乗りください。
… ban no basu ni onori kudasai
you need to get the number … bus

この列車は … に停車いたします。
kono ressha wa … ni têsha itashimasu
this train calls at …

二つ先のバス停
futatsu saki no basu tê
two stops from here

BY CAR

You will need an International Driving Permit to drive in Japan. They drive on the left and there are right of way signs at every junction. If you see 止まれ *tomare*, either written on the road or on a roadsign, it is equivalent to a STOP sign. Speed limits are 100 km/h on motorways and 60 km/h on other types of road. Built-up areas often have a 20 km/h limit. Motorway tolls are very expensive and there is almost always a charge for street parking.

You can spot taxis by the sign on the roof, bearing the name of the taxi company. Inside, the seats have white protective covers and the drivers wear white gloves. A small sign by the driver's window indicates whether the taxi is free (空車 *kûsha*). Doors open and close automatically, so you should not try to do this yourself. Standard taxis (中型 *chûgata*) take a maximum of four passengers, but the smaller ones (小型 *kogata*) only take three. If you are going somewhere other than well-known locations, such as big hotels and tourist attractions, it is useful to have directions or a map, as taxi-drivers usually have less detailed knowledge of their cities than in Britain.

Expressing yourself

where can I find a service station?
ガソリンスタンドはどこにありますか。
gasorin sutando wa doko ni arimasu ka?

lead-free petrol, please
無鉛をお願いします。
muen o onegai shimasu

how much is it per litre?
１リットルいくらですか。
ichi rittoru ikura desu ka?

we got stuck in a traffic jam
交通渋滞に巻き込まれました。
kôtsûjûtai ni makikomaremashita

I've broken down
車が故障しました。
kuruma ga koshô shimashita

is there a garage near here?
この近くに自動車修理工場はありますか。
kono chikaku ni jidôsha shûrikôjô wa arimasen ka?

can you help us to push the car?
車を押してもらえませんか。
kuruma o oshite moraemasen ka?

the battery's dead
バッテリーがあがってしまいました。
batterî ga agatte shimaimashita

we've run out of petrol
ガス欠になりました。
gasu ketsu ni narimashita

I've got a puncture
パンクしてしまいました。
panku shite shimaimashita

we've just had an accident
事故にあいました。
jiko ni aimashita

I've lost my car keys
車の鍵を失くしてしまいました。
kuruma no kagi o nakushite shimaimashita

how long will it take to repair?
修理にどれくらい時間がかかりますか。
shûri ni dore kurai jikan ga kakarimasu ka?

◆ Hiring a car

I'd like to hire a car for a week
車を1週間、借りたいんですが。
kuruma o isshûkan karitai n desu ga

an automatic (car)
オートマチック車
ôtomachikku sha

I'd like to take out comprehensive insurance
総合自動車保険に入りたいんですが。
sôgô jidôsha hoken ni hairitai n desu ga

◆ Getting a taxi

is there a taxi rank near here?
この近くにタクシー乗り場はありますか。
kono chikaku ni takushî noriba wa arimasu ka?

I'd like to go to …
… までお願いします。
… made onegai shimasu

I'd like to book a taxi for 8 o'clock
タクシーを8時に予約したいんですが。
takushî o hachi ji ni yoyaku shitai n desu ga

you can drop me off here, thanks
ここで降ろしてください。ありがとう。
koko de oroshite kudasai. arigatô

how much will it be to go to the airport?
空港までいくらですか。
kûkô made ikura desu ka?

◆ Hitchhiking

I'm going to …
… に行くつもりです。
… ni iku tsumori desu

could you take me as far as …?
… まで乗せてくれませんか。
… made nosete kuremasen ka?

thanks for the lift
乗せてもらって助かりました。
nosete moratte tasukarimashita

can you drop me off here?
ここで降ろしてくれませんか。
koko de oroshite kuremasen ka?

we hitched a lift
ヒッチハイクをして来ました。
hitchihaiku o shite kimashita

Understanding

満車 *mansha*	full (*in car park*)
スペース有 *supêsuari*	spaces (*in car park*)
チケットをお持ちください。 *chiketto o omochi kudasai*	keep your ticket
レンタカー *rentakâ*	car hire
駐車場 *chûshajô*	car park
徐行 *jokô*	slow
駐車禁止 *chûsa kinshi*	no parking
走行車線変更 *sôkô shasen*	get in lane
制限速度 *sêgen sokudu*	speed limit
料金所 *ryôkinjo*	toll

免許証と身分証明書、クレジットカードをお見せください。
menkyoshô to mibunshômeisho, kurejitto kâdo o omise kudasai
I'll need your driving licence, proof of address and your credit card

保証金は 1 万円 です。
hoshôkin wa ichiman en desu
there's a 10,000-yen deposit

分かりました、乗ってください。… まで乗せましょう。
wakarimashita. notte kudasai … made nosemashô.
all right, get in, I'll take you as far as …

BY BOAT

As Japan is an archipelago, travel by sea has always been very important. Now there are various bridges and tunnels which make life easier for drivers, but ferries are still popular, particularly on the Aomori–Hokkaidô and Honshû–Kyûshû lines. There are tourist boat trips out to the most famous islands (Miyajima, Kashikojima etc).

Expressing yourself

how long is the crossing?
渡るのにどれくらい時間がかかりますか。
wataru no ni dore kurai jikan ga kakarimasu ka?

I'm seasick
船酔いしました。
funayoi shimashita

Understanding

車なしでお乗りのお客様 *kuruma nashi de onori no okyaku-sama*	foot passengers only
次の便は … です *tsugi no bin wa… desu*	next crossing at …

If you are planning to visit during the holiday periods of **Golden Week** (end of April to beginning of May) or mid-August, or during the New Year period, you should book your accommodation several months in advance. You generally only pay when you get there. It is always a good idea to contact the Japanese Tourist Information Office for advice.

Ryokan are traditional Japanese hotels: rooms are furnished with futons and **tatami** mats, and the food is traditional Japanese. Bathrooms are usually communal (but single-sex) and contain a huge **ofuro** (a pool which you only get into after washing thoroughly), often with natural hot spring water (**onsen**). Prices are usually per person rather than per room, and can be up to around 30,000 yen. Charges usually include breakfast and dinner in traditional **ryokan**.

Large hotel chains like Prince Hotel, Miyako Hotel and Tokyu are found in big cities, seaside resorts and ski resorts, and offer similar service to what you would expect back home. Prices are usually slightly higher than a **ryokan**.

In rural areas, there is the option of staying in a small, family-run house, rather like a bed and breakfast. These can be Western-style (a **penshon**) or Japanese (a **minshuku**).

Youth hostels are not particularly cheap, costing around 3,000–3,500 yen per person per night in a single-sex dormitory. You need to have a Youth Hostel Membership Card, and you can join at any hostel in Japan if you aren't already a member.

If you are planning a long stay, look for a **gaijin house** ("house for foreigners"). The monthly rent is reasonable and includes electricity, water and gas. There is no deposit.

There are plenty of campsites, but camping out in the open is strictly forbidden.

The basics

bath	（お）風呂 (o)furo
bathroom	風呂場 furo ba
bathroom with shower	シャワー付き shawâ tsuki
bed	ベッド beddo
bed and breakfast	朝食付き chôshoku tsuki
cable television	ケーブルテレビ kêburu terebi
campsite	キャンプ場 kyampu jô
caravan	キャンピングカー kyampingu kâ
cottage	貸しロッジ kashi rojji
double bed	ダブルベッド daburu beddo
double room	ダブルルーム daburu rûmu
en-suite bathroom	バス、トイレ付 basu, toire tsuki
family room	ファミリールーム famirî rûmu
flat	アパート apâto
full-board	3食付 san shoku tsuki
fully inclusive	全込み zenbu komi
half-board	2食付 ni shoku tsuki
hotel	ホテル hoteru
key	鍵 kagi
rent	家賃 yachin
self-catering	自炊 jisui
shower	シャワー shawâ
single bed	シングルベッド shinguru beddo
single room	シングルルーム shinguru rûmu
tenant	借家人 shakuyanin
tent	テント tento
toilets	トイレ toire, お手洗い otearai
youth hostel	ユースホステル yûsu hosuteru
to book	予約する yoyaku suru
to rent	借りる kariru
to reserve	予約する yoyaku suru

ACCOMMODATION

Expressing yourself

I have a reservation
予約してあります。
yoyaku shite arimasu

the name's ...
名前は ... です。
namae wa ... desu

do you take credit cards?
クレジットカードで払えますか。
kurejitto kâdo de haraemasu ka?

Understanding

空室 *kûshitsu*	vacancies
満室 *manshitsu*	full
立入禁止 *tachi-iri kinshi*	private
受付 *uketsuke*, フロント *furonto*	reception
お手洗い *otearai*, トイレ *toire*	toilets

パスポートを見せていただけますか。
pasupôto o misete itadakemasu ka?
could I see your passport, please?

この用紙にご記入ください。
kono yôshi ni gokinyû kudasai
could you fill in this form?

HOTELS

Expressing yourself

do you have any vacancies?
部屋はありますか。
heya wa arimasu ka?

how much is a double room per night?
ダブルルームは一泊いくらですか。
daburu rûmu wa ippaku ikura desu ka?

I'd like to reserve a double room/a single room
ダブルルーム・シングルルームを予約したいんですが。
daburu rûmu/shinguru rûmu o yoyaku shitai n desu ga

for three nights
3泊。
sampaku

would it be possible to stay an extra night?
もう一晩泊まれますか。
mô hitoban tomaremasu ka?

do you have any rooms available for tonight?
今夜、部屋は空いていますか。
komban, heya wa aite imasu ka?

do you have any family rooms?
ファミリールームはありますか。
famirî rûmu wa arimasu ka?

would it be possible to add an extra bed?
もうひとつベッドを入れてもらえますか。
mô hitotsu beddo o irete moraemasu ka?

could I see the room first?
先に部屋も見せてもらえますか。
saki ni heyao misete moraemasu ka?

do you have anything bigger/quieter?
もっと大きな・静かな部屋はありますか。
motto ôkina/shizukana heya wa arimasu ka?

that's fine, I'll take it
これでいいです。お願いします。
kore de î desu. onegai shimasu

could you recommend any other hotels?
他のホテルを紹介してくれますか。
hoka no hoteru o shôkai shite kuremasu ka?

is breakfast included?
朝食は含まれていますか。
chôshoku wa fukumarete imasu ka?

what time do you serve breakfast?
朝食は何時ですか。
chôshoku wa nan ji desu ka?

is there a lift?
エレベーターはありますか。
erebêtâ wa arimasu ka?

is the hotel near the centre of town?
ホテルは町の中心に近いですか。
hoteru wa machi no chûshin ni chikai desu ka?

what time will the room be ready?
何時に部屋に入れますか。
nan ji ni heya ni hairemasu ka?

the key for room ..., please
… 号室の鍵をください。
... gô shitsu no kagi o kudasai

could I have an extra blanket?
毛布をもう一枚もらえますか。
môfu o mô ichi mai moraemasu ka

the air conditioning/heating isn't working
エアコン・ヒーターが効きません。
eakon/hîtâ ga kikimasen

Understanding

申し訳ありませんが、満室です。
môshiwake arimasen ga, manshitsu desu
I'm sorry, but we're full

シングルルームしかございません。
shinguru rûmu shika gozaimasen
we only have a single room available

何泊でしょうか。
nampaku deshô ka?
how many nights is it for?

お名前はなんとおっしゃいますか。
onamae wa nan to osshaimasu ka?
what's your name, please?

チェックインは正午からです。
chekkuin wa shôgo kara desu
check-in is from midday

11時までにチェックアウトをお願いいたします。
jûichi ji made ni chekkuauto o onegai shimasu
you have to check out before 11am

朝食はレストランで7時半から9時までです。
chôshoku wa resutoran de shichi ji han kara ku ji made desu
breakfast is served in the restaurant between 7.30 and 9.00

朝、新聞をお届けいたしましょうか。
asa, shimbun o otodoke itashimashô ka?
would you like a newspaper in the morning?

まだ部屋の準備ができτおりません。
mada heya no jumbi ga dekite orimasen
your room isn't ready yet

荷物はここに置いていただいて結構です。
nimotsu wa koko ni oite itadaite kekkô desu
you can leave your bags here

ミニバーはお使いになりましたか。
minibâ wa otsukai ni narimashita ka?
have you used the minibar?

YOUTH HOSTELS

Expressing yourself

do you have space for two people for tonight?
今夜、二人分空いていますか。
kon'ya futari bun aite imasu ka?

ACCOMMODATION

we've booked two beds for three nights
二人分、三泊の予約をしてあります。
futari bun, sampaku no yoyaku o shite arimasu

could I leave my backpack at reception?
バックパックを受付で預かってもらえますか。
bakkupakku o uketsuke de azukatte moraemasu ka?

do you have somewhere we could leave our bikes?
自転車を置く所はありますか。
jitensha o oku tokoro wa arimasu ka?

I'll come back for it around 7 o'clock
7時ごろ戻ってきます。
shichi ji goro modotte kimasu

there's no hot water
お湯が出ません。
oyu ga demasen

the sink's blocked
シンクが詰まっています。
shinku ga tsumatte imasu

Understanding

会員証はお持ちですか。
kai-in shô wa omochi desu ka?
do you have a membership card?

シーツはお貸しします。
shîtsu wa okashi shimasu
bed linen is provided

ホステルは午後6時に開きます。
hosuteru wa gogo roku ji ni akimasu
the hostel reopens at 6pm

SELF-CATERING

Expressing yourself

we're looking for somewhere to rent near a town
町に近いところを探しています。
machi ni chikai tokoro o sagashite imasu

where do we pick up/leave the keys?
鍵はどこで受け取ればいいですか。・どこに返せばいいですか?
kagi wa doko de uketoreba î desu ka?/doko ni kaeseba î desu ka?

is electricity included in the price?
電気代は料金に含まれていますか。
denki dai wa ryôkin ni fukumarete imasu ka?

are bed linen and towels provided?
シーツとタオルは貸してもらえますか。
shîtsu to taoru wa kashite moraemasu ka?

is a car necessary?
車が要りますか。
kuruma ga irimasu ka?

is the accommodation suitable for elderly people?
高齢者・お年寄りも利用しやすいですか。
kôrêsha/otoshiyori mo riyô shiyasui desu ka?

where is the nearest supermarket?
近いスーパーはどこですか。
chikai sûpâ wa doko desu ka?

Understanding

出発の前に家を掃除し、片付けてください。
shuppatsu no mae ni ie o sôji shi, katazukete kudasai
please leave the house clean and tidy when you leave

家具付です。
kagu tsuki desu
the house is fully furnished

料金に全て含まれています。
ryôkin ni subete fukumarete imasu
everything is included in the price

このあたりでは、車がどうしても必要です。
kono atari de wa, kuruma ga dôshite mo hitsuyô desu
you really need a car in this part of the country

CAMPING

Expressing yourself

is there a campsite near here?
この近くにキャンプ場はありますか。
kono chikaku ni kyampu jô wa arimasu ka

I'd like to book a space for a two-person tent for three nights
二人用テントの場所を３泊予約したいんですが。
futari yô tento no basho o sampaku yoyaku shitai n desu ga

how much is it a night?
一晩いくらですか。
hitoban ikura desu ka?

where is the shower block?
シャワー室はどこですか。
shawâ shitsu wa doko desu ka?

can we pay, please? we were at space ...
支払いをしたいんですが。場所は ... です。
shiharai o shitai n desu ga, basho wa ... desu

Understanding

お一人様、一晩につき ... です。
ohitori sama, hitoban ni tsuki ... desu
it's ... per person per night

何か御用がおありでしたら、いらっしゃってください。
nani ka goyô ga oari deshitara, irasshatte kudasai
if you need anything, just come and ask

EATING AND DRINKING

There are an enormous variety of eating places in Japan, from inexpensive fast-food joints like **Mos Burger** and **Yoshinoya**, or noodle or sushi bars, to high-quality establishments serving Japanese or Western food – it's best to visit these in the company of a local. Almost everywhere is open nonstop from 10am to 10pm. Most restaurants specialize in a particular type of food (eels, fried pork, noodles, sushi etc) and offer good deals (set menus) at lunchtime.

Green tea is served rather than water with Japanese food.

You generally pay at the exit, in cash, and there is no need to leave a tip.

The basics

beer	ビール *bîru*
bill	勘定書き *kanjôgaki*
black coffee	ブラックコーヒー *burakku kôhî*
bottle	びん *bin*
bread	パン *pan*
breakfast	朝食 *chôshoku*, 朝ごはん *asagohan*
coffee	コーヒー *kôhî*
Coke®	コーラ *kôra*
dessert	デザート *dezâto*
dinner	夕食 *yûshoku*, 夕飯 *yûhan*, 晩ごはん *bangohan*
fruit juice	フルーツジュース *furûtsu jûsu*
lemonade	レモネード *remonêdo*
lunch	昼食 *chûshoku*, 昼ごはん *hirugohan*
main course	メインコース *mên kôsu*
menu	メニュー *menyû*
mineral water	ミネラルウォーター *mineraru wôtâ*
order	注文 *chûmon*
red wine	赤ワイン *aka wain*
rosé wine	ロゼ *roze*
salad	サラダ *sarada*

sandwich	サンドイッチ *sandoitchi*
service	サービス *sâbisu*
set menu	定食 *têshoku*
sparkling	*(water, wine)* 発泡性の *happôsê no*
starter	前菜 *zensai*
still	*(water)* ガスなし *gasu nashi*
tea	*(green)* お茶 *ocha*; *(black)* 紅茶 *kôcha*
water	水 *mizu*
white coffee	カフェオーレ *kafe ôre*
white wine	白ワイン *shiro wain*
wine	ワイン *wain*
wine list	ワインリスト *wain risuto*
to eat	食べる *taberu*
to have breakfast	朝食・朝ごはんを食べる *chôshoku/asagohan o taberu*
to have dinner	夕食・夕飯を食べる *yûshoku/yûhan o taberu*
to have lunch	昼食・昼ごはんを食べる *chûshoku/hirugohan o taberu*
to order	注文する *chûmon suru*

Expressing yourself

shall we go and have something to eat?
どこかへ食事に行きましょうか。
doko ka e shokuji ni ikimashô ka?

do you want to go for a drink?
飲みに行きませんか。
nomi ni ikimasen ka?

can you recommend a good restaurant?
いいレストランを教えてくれませんか。
î resutoran o oshiete kuremasen ka?

I'm not very hungry
あまり、おなかがすいていません。
amari onaka ga suite imasen

excuse me! *(to call the waiter)*
すみません
sumimasen!

cheers!
乾杯
kampai!

that was lovely
とてもおいしかったです。
totemo oishikatta desu

could you bring us an ashtray, please?
灰皿をください。
haizara o kudasai

where are the toilets, please?
お手洗い・トイレはどこですか。
otearai/toire wa doko desu ka?

could I have a knife and fork, please?
ナイフとフォークをもらえませんか。
naifu to fôku o moraemasen ka?

Understanding

おしぼり *oshibori*   small moistened towel
お持ち帰り *omochikaeri*   takeaway

いただきます。
itadakimasu
= set phrase said before a meal, roughly equivalent to "I gratefully receive"

ごちそうさま。
gochisôsama
= set phrase said after a meal, roughly equivalent to "thank you for the meal"

申し訳ございません。11時で終わりになります。
môshiwake gozaimasen. jûichi ji de owari ni narimasu
I'm sorry, we stop serving at 11pm

RESERVING A TABLE

Expressing yourself

I'd like to reserve a table for tomorrow evening
明日の晩の予約をしたいんですが。
ashita no ban no yoyaku o shitai n desu ga

for two people
二人分。
futari bun

around 8 o'clock
8時頃。
hachi ji goro

do you have a table available any earlier than that?
それより早い時間に空いている席はありませんか。
sore yori hayai jikan ni aite iru seki wa arimasen ka?

I've reserved a table – the name's …
席を予約してあります。名前は … です。
seki o yoyaku shite arimasu. namae wa … desu

Understanding

予約席 *yoyaku seki*
reserved

何時でしょうか。
nan ji deshô ka?
for what time?

何名様でしょうか。
nam mê sama deshô ka?
for how many people?

お名前は。
onamae wa?
what's the name?

タバコはお吸いになりますか。
tabako wa osui ni narimasu ka?
smoking or non-smoking?

予約はしていらっしゃいますか。
yoyaku wa shite irasshaimasu ka?
do you have a reservation?

あの隅のテーブルでよろしいでしょうか。
ano sumi no têburu de yoroshî deshô ka?
is this table in the corner OK for you?

申し訳ございません、いっぱいです。
môshiwake gozaimasen, ippai desu
I'm afraid we're full at the moment

ORDERING FOOD

Expressing yourself

yes, we're ready to order
はい、決まりました。
hai, kimarimashita

no, could you give us a few more minutes?
もう少し待ってくれますか。
mô sukoshi matte kuremasu ka?

I'd like …
… をお願いします。
… o onegai shimasu

could I have …?
… をもらえますか。
… o moraemasu ka?

I'm not sure, what's "soba"?
よく分からないんですが、そばって何ですか。
yoku wakaranai n desu ga, soba tte nan desu ka?

I'll have that
あれにします。
are ni shimasu

does it come with vegetables?
野菜はついてきますか。
yasai wa tsuite kimasu ka?

what are today's specials?
今日のお奨めは何ですか。
kyô no osusume wa nan desu ka?

what desserts do you have?
デザートはどんなものがありますか。
dezâto wa donna mono ga arimasu ka?

I'm allergic to nuts/wheat/seafood/citrus fruit
ナッツ・小麦・魚介類・かんきつ類にアレルギーがあります。
nattsu/komugi/gyokairui/kankitsurui ni arerugî ga arimasu

EATING AND DRINKING

some water, please
お水をください。
omizu o kudasai

a bottle of red/white wine
赤・白ワインを一本。
aka/shiro wain o ippon

that's for me
それは私のです。
sore wa watashi no desu

this isn't what I ordered, I wanted …
私が注文したのはそれじゃありません。… です。
watashi ga chûmon shita no wa sore ja arimasen … desu

could we have some more tea, please?
お茶をもう少しもらえますか。
ocha o mô sukoshi moraemasu ka?

could you bring us another jug of water, please?
お水をもっとください。
omizu o motto kudasai

Understanding

ご注文はお決まりでしょうか。
gochûmon wa okimari deshô ka?
are you ready to order?

少ししてから、また参ります。
sukoshi shite kara, mata mairimasu
I'll come back in a few minutes

申し訳ございません。… は終わってしまいました。
môshiwake gozaimasen … wa owatte shimaimashita
I'm sorry, we don't have any … left

お飲みものは何になさいますか。
onomimono wa nan ni nasaimasu ka?
what would you like to drink?

デザートかコーヒーはいかがですか。
dezâto ka kôhî wa ikaga desu ka?
would you like dessert or coffee?

いかがでしたか。
ikaga deshita ka?
was everything OK?

BARS AND CAFÉS

Traditional drinking establishments vary from traditional Japanese bars (**izakaya**) to modern manga cafés, not forgetting the classic tea salons and hostess bars. Alcohol plays a strategic role in Japanese culture, loosening tongues and helping to shake off some of the social constraints – in fact, going to the **izakaya** or **sunakku** (western-style bar) is an essential part of life for any self-respecting businessman. People generally go out between about 9pm and midnight. The legal drinking age in Japan is 20.

Coffee shops/cafés (**kissaten**) serve western-style cakes and light meals as well as drinks, and many have a particular style and accompanying music (for example, jazz or classical). They can be quite expensive, but you can take your time there and enjoy the atmosphere. A **môningu setto** (morning set) is a good deal for breakfast: tea or coffee and toast, sometimes with a hard-boiled egg. Chains such as Starbucks and Mr Donuts and the Japanese Doutor are now common and much cheaper than the **kissaten**.

Expressing yourself

I'd like ...
... にします。
... ni shimasu

a Coke®/a diet Coke®
コーラ・ダイエットコーラ。
kôra/daietto kôra

a glass of white/red wine
白・赤のグラスワイン。
shiro/aka no gurasu wain

EATING AND DRINKING

a black/white coffee
ブラックコーヒー・カフェオーレ。
burakku kôhî/kafe ôre

a cup of tea
紅茶。
kôcha

a coffee and toast
コーヒーとトースト。
kôhî to tôsuto

a cup of hot chocolate
ココア。
kokoa

the same again, please
同じものをお願いします。
onaji mono o onegai shimasu

a morning set, please
モーニングセットをお願いします。
môningu setto o onegai shimasu

Understanding

アルコールなしの *arukôru nashi no* non-alcoholic

何を召し上がりますか。
nani o meshiagarimasu ka?
what would you like?

ここは禁煙席でございます。
koko wa kin'en seki de gozaimasu
this is the non-smoking area

今、お支払いいただけますか。
ima, oshiharai itadakemasu ka?
could I ask you to pay now, please?

Some informal expressions

おなかいっぱい。 *onaka ippai* I'm full
おなかぺこぺこ。 *onaka pekopeko* I'm starving
酔っ払っちゃった。 *yopparatchatta* I'm drunk
二日酔いだ。 *futsukayoi da* I have a hangover

THE BILL

Expressing yourself

the bill, please
お勘定、お願いします。
okanjô onegai shimasu

how much do I owe you?
おいくらですか。
oikura desu ka?

do you take credit cards?
クレジットカードで払えますか。
kurejitto kâdo de haraemasu ka?

I think there's a mistake in the bill
計算が間違っているんじゃないかと思うんですが。
kêsan ga machigatte iru n ja nai ka to omou n desu ga

is service included?
サービス料込みですか。
sâbisu ryô komi desu ka?

can we pay separately?
別々に払えますか。
betsubetsu ni haraemasu ka?

let's split the bill
割り勘にしましょう。
warikan ni shimashô

Understanding

お会計はご一緒にされますか。
okaikê wa goissho ni saremasu ka?
are you all paying together?

はい、サービス料込みです。
hai, sâbisu ryô komi desu
yes, service is included

FOOD AND DRINK

Unlike European cooking, where the emphasis is on mixing ingredients together, Japanese food is all about juxtaposing different elements. It is very refined, and the delicious flavours are matched by careful presentation.

A traditional Japanese breakfast (usually served from 7am) would include rice (often with a raw egg mixed into it), **miso shiru** (soup made with fermented soya bean paste), **nori** (seaweed), **tôfu** (soya bean curd) and fermented soya beans (**nattô**) and dried fish. However, continental-style breakfasts of coffee, bread and jam are becoming increasingly common. Lunch is often a quick snack, eaten between 12 and 1pm in an inexpensive restaurant. The traditional packed lunch known as **bentô** is still very popular, whether homemade, bought in the street or from a **kombini** (convenience store). Work conditions permitting, families usually get together at about 7pm for a substantial evening meal.

Japanese people rarely ate meat until the Meiji period (1868–1912), although they did eat fish and birds. However, vegetarianism (**saishoku shugi**) is not common in Japan today, despite the long tradition of Buddhist vegetarian food (**shôjin ryôri**). Many Japanese dishes contain small amounts of fish or meat (particularly ham or bacon, which may not be considered as meat), and bonito fish flakes are used in stock for soup and other dishes. You can try asking for a dish without X (X **nashi**).

Understanding

ゆでた yudeta	boiled
パン粉をまぶした panko o mabushita	breaded
こんがり焼いた kongari yaita	browned
炭火で焼いた sumibi de yaita	charcoal-grilled
冷たい tsumetai	cold, chilled
揚げた ageta	deep-fried
角切りにした kakugiri ni shita	diced

乾燥させた kansô saseta	dried
詰めた tsumeta	filled, stuffed
辛い karai	hot, spicy
ミディアムの midiamu no	medium *(steak)*
溶かした tokashita	melted
オーブンで焼いた ôbun de yaita	oven-roasted
レアの rea no	rare *(steak)*
スライスした suraisu shita	sliced
薫製の kunsê no	smoked
炒めた itameta	stir-fried
甘い amai	sweet
ウェルダンの werudan no	well done *(steak)*

◆ Condiments, spices and pickles

塩 shio	salt
コショウ koshô	pepper
醤油 shôyu	soya sauce
味噌 miso	fermented soya bean paste
酢 su	Japanese vinegar (a little sweet)
ワサビ wasabi	horseradish mustard (bright green and very hot!)
漬け物 tsukemono	pickles (cucumber, white radish, turnip, Chinese leaves etc pickled in salt, soya sauce, vinegar, *miso* etc)
紅しょうが beni shôga	sliced pickled ginger pickled in vinegar
梅干 umeboshi	pickled plum
油 abura	oil
ごま油 goma abura	sesame oil
オリーブオイル orîbu oiru	olive oil

◆ Rice and rice-based dishes

Rice is the staple food in Japan. You will be served a bowl of rice with every meal and you can also find it pressed into triangular shapes (**onigiri**), wrapped in **nori** seaweed, or in **sushi**. The suffix **don** at the end of the name of a dish means that it will be served on a bowl of plain white rice (**katsudon**, **gyûdon**, **tendon** etc). The **bentô** (lunchbox) makes an ideal packed lunch or picnic. A traditional Japanese wife or mother is expected to make them for her husband or children each morning. They can be bought in small shops and station kiosks.

ご飯 gohan	boiled white rice
米 kome	rice (uncooked)
玄米 gemmai	brown rice
おにぎり onigiri	rice ball wrapped in nori seaweed and containing various fillings, such as a pickled plum, salmon or seaweed.
弁当 bentô	lunchbox with rice and a variety of other foods
海苔 nori	sheets of dried seaweed, used to wrap sushi and onigiri; also cut up fine and scattered on dishes
どんぶり domburi	large bowl of rice with various toppings
カツ丼 katsudon	large bowl of rice topped with breaded deep-fried pork cutlet
牛丼 gyûdon	large bowl of rice topped with fine slices of beef with soya sauce
天丼 tendon	large bowl of rice topped with battered and deep-fried vegetables, fish and prawns (tempura)
親子丼 oyakodon	large bowl of rice topped with chicken and lightly scrambled egg
卵丼 tamagodon	large bowl of rice topped with lightly scrambled egg and vegetables
五目ご飯 gomoku gohan	warm rice mixed with shredded vegetables, eggs etc
チャーハン châhan	fried rice, usually containing meat and vegetables
お茶漬け ochazuke	rice on which hot green tea is poured
オムライス omuraisu	rice with tomato ketchup wrapped in an omelette
お粥 okayu	rice porridge given to the elderly and ill
もち mochi	sticky rice cakes eaten either with soya sauce or with sweetened azuki bean paste

◆ Soups and stews

Unlike **nabe**, which is similar to a stew and is a meal in itself, miso soup usually comes as part of a meal.

味噌汁 *miso shiru*	miso soup, based on different kinds of fermented soya bean paste. The ingredients, including vegetables, seaweed, shellfish or tofu (bean curd), may change according to the seasons and different regions have their own specialities.
鍋料理 *nabe ryôri*	stew with vegetables, pork or beef, fish or shellfish
ちゃんこ鍋 *chanko nabe*	hearty stew of meat and vegetables, famous for being served to sumo wrestlers

◆ Fruit and vegetables

Fruit and vegetables are different in size and kind from those in the UK and the US. Organic fruit and vegetables are still quite rare. The **daikon** (a large white radish at least 30cm long) is an important vegetable in Japanese cuisine, eaten cooked in miso soup or in slices, or raw in salad, or grated and mixed into soya sauce. Cabbage (**kyabetsu**) is also common, shredded as a salad. Potatoes (**jagaimo**) feature particularly in a dish beloved of children, **karê raisu** (curry rice), which consists of meat, potatoes and carrots in a thick mild curry sauce, similar to Chinese takeaway curry in Britain, and served with rice. Sweet potatoes (**satsumaimo**) are popular, traditionally sold by street vendors with carts in the winter.

Fruit is cultivated, selected and presented with great care, often grown to much larger sizes than in the UK or US and commanding exorbitant prices. Fruit is usually peeled when served, including grapes.

根菜 *konsai*	root vegetables
大根 *daikon*	white radish
ニンジン *ninjin*	carrot

FOOD AND DRINK

タマネギ *tamanegi*	onion
ネギ *negi*	spring onion
ゴボウ *gobô*	burdock
ジャガイモ *jagaimo*	potato
サツマイモ *satsumaimo*	sweet potato
サトイモ *satoimo*	taro
緑黄色野菜 *ryokuôshoku yasai*	green vegetables
キャベツ *kyabetsu*	cabbage
カリフラワー *karifurawâ*	cauliflower
白菜 *hakusai*	Chinese leaves
ナス *nasu*	aubergine
ズッキーニ *zukkîni*	courgette
キュウリ *kyûri*	cucumber
ほうれん草 *hôrensô*	spinach
かぼちゃ *kabocha*	pumpkin
竹の子 *takenoko*	bamboo shoots
きのこ *kinoko*	mushroom
椎茸 *shîtake*	Japanese brown mushroom with a strong taste, commonly available dried
シメジ *shimeji*	grey-brown beech mushroom with long stalk
松茸 *matsutake*	pine mushroom, much sought-after and very expensive
エノキ *enoki*	Chinese hackberry mushroom (small white long-stalked mushroom)
ナメコ *nameko*	small orange-gold gelatinous mushroom
豆 *mame*	bean
サヤインゲン *saya ingen*	green bean
インゲン豆 *ingen mame*	haricot bean
グリンピース *gurinpîsu*	peas
そら豆 *sora mame*	broad bean
大豆 *daizu*	soya bean
種 *tane*	seed, nut, grain
ごま *goma*	sesame
栗 *kuri*	chestnut
果物 *kudamono*	fruit
フルーツ *furûtsu*	fruit
トマト *tomato*	tomato
レモン *remon*	lemon

オレンジ *orenji*	orange
ミカン *mikan*	satsuma, clementine, mandarin
グレープフルーツ *gurêpufurûtsu*	grapefruit
ブドウ *budô*	grape
リンゴ *ringo*	apple
梨 *nashi*	Japanese pear
柿 *kaki*	persimmon
メロン *meron*	melon
苺 *ichigo*	strawberry
梅 *ume*	plum

◆ Meat

Meat is very popular in Japan, and is served in a variety of ways: in fondues (**sukiyaki**), on skewers, breaded and deep-fried or even raw.

Small pieces of meat are cooked on bamboo skewers and grilled over a wood fire – they do not generally come with rice, but you can order it separately in the form of **onigiri** (see the section on rice).

Fondues are prepared at the table. First a kind of stock is made in a cast iron pot, and vegetables and then **tôfu** are added little by little. Then small strips of raw meat are dipped into the pot to be cooked.

肉 *niku*	meat
… の肉 *… no niku*	… meat
牛肉 *gyûniku*, ビーフ *bîfu*	beef
松阪牛 *matsuzaka gyû*	high-quality beef, known abroad as Kobe beef
豚肉 *butaniku*, ポーク *pôku*	pork
鶏肉 *toriniku*, チキン *chikin*	chicken
馬肉 *baniku*, さくら肉 *sakuraniku*	horsemeat (*served raw or smoked, a speciality of the Shinshû region*)
鹿の肉 *shika no niku*	venison (*served raw or in stew, popular in northern Japan*)

猪の肉 *inoshishi no niku*, ぼたん *botan*	boar meat
ハム *hamu*	ham
ベーコン *bêkon*	bacon
焼き鳥 *yakitori*	grilled chicken on a skewer
焼き肉 *yakiniku*	grilled meat
串カツ *kushikatsu*	pieces of pork and vegetables, breaded and deep-fried, served on a skewer *(a speciality of Osaka)*
ミートボール *mîto bôru*	meatballs
すき焼き *sukiyaki*	beef, tofu and vegetables cooked fondue-style at the table and dipped in beaten raw egg
しゃぶしゃぶ *shabushabu*	thinly sliced beef and vegetables cooked fondue-style at the table in a fish and seaweed stock and dipped in a sauce based on soya sauce and flavoured with citrus juice, sesame seeds and other flavourings

◆ Eggs

卵 *tamago*	egg
生卵 *nama tamago*	raw egg
ゆで卵 *yude tamago*	hard-boiled egg
半熟卵 *hanjuku tamago*	soft-boiled egg
卵焼き *tamago yaki*	slices of rolled sweet omelette flavoured with soya sauce, served on *sushi* and in *bentô* lunchboxes
目玉焼き *medama yaki*	fried egg
温泉卵 *onsen tamago*	coddled egg served in broth made of fish stock, soya sauce and *mirin* (sweetened rice wine)
オムレツ *omuretsu*	omelette
茶碗蒸し *chawan mushi*	savoury egg custard with vegetables, quail's egg, mushrooms etc served in a small lidded bowl
ウズラの卵 *uzura no tamago*	quail's egg

FOOD AND DRINK

◆ Deep-fried food

Tempura, battered and deep-fried fish and vegetables, is one of the rare traditional dishes which originates in the West: cooking in oil was introduced by the Portuguese in the 16th century. **Tempura têshoku** (tempura set meal) consists of an assortment of five or six pieces of fish, prawns and vegetables served on a paper napkin; these are dipped in a sauce made of soya sauce mixed with grated **daikon** (white radish). Miso soup, rice and pickles are served with them.

天ぷら tempura	deep-fried fish, prawns and vegetables
トンカツ tonkatsu	breaded pork cutlet
エビフライ ebi furai	breaded and deep-fried prawns
カキフライ kaki furai	breaded and deep-fried oysters
コロッケ korokke	potato and mincemeat croquettes

◆ Soya

Soya is another essential part of the Japanese diet, and a very healthy one, as it is low in calories and high in protein. It is the basis of all the vegetarian dishes cooked by the Buddhist monks (**shôjin ryôri**). It comes in many forms: as a sauce (**shôyu**), as fermented beans (**nattô**), as blocks of bean curd (**tôfu**) or as a thick paste of fermented beans (**miso**). **Tôfu** is eaten either as it is or in soup, depending on the season. It is also served cold, sprinkled with ginger and garnished with finely chopped spring onion and soya sauce, or deep-fried.

しょう油 shôyu	soya sauce
味噌 miso	fermented soya bean paste
豆腐 tôfu	bean curd
冷や奴 hiyayakko	cold bean curd
揚げ出し豆腐 agedashidôfu	deep-fried bean curd
納豆 nattô	fermented soya beans
もやし moyashi	bean sprouts

FOOD AND DRINK

枝豆 *edamame*	fresh green soya beans boiled and lightly salted and served with beer (to be removed from their pods)
豆乳 *tônyû*	soya milk
精進料理 *shôjin ryôri*	Buddhist monks' vegetarian cuisine

◆ Raw fish and seafood

There is a huge variety of fish available in Japan, some of which is not found in the West. It is often eaten raw (**sashimi**). Freshness is strictly controlled both in restaurants and supermarkets. In specialized restaurants (すし屋 **sushiya**), the price of sushi varies considerably according to whether dishes are presented on a conveyor belt or ordered from a menu. With the latter, food can be extremely high quality – but with prices to match. A **moriawase**, or typical selection, usually includes 18 pieces. In a **kaitenzushi**, you pick up dishes as they pass you on a conveyor belt, then pile the empty plates up next to you. The bill is calculated based on the number and colour of plates you end up with.

刺身 *sashimi*	slices of raw fish dipped in soya sauce flavoured with *wasabi* (hot green horseradish sauce)
にぎり寿司 *nigirizushi*	slices of fish, seafood or omelette on small blocks of lightly vinegared rice (sushi)
巻き寿司 *makizushi*	rice filled with fish, omelette, mushrooms etc, wrapped in *nori* seaweed and sliced
ちらし寿司 *chirashi zushi*	scattered sushi (cold, slightly vinegared rice with carrots, cucumber, mushrooms, fish, strips of omelette, *nori* seaweed etc scattered on top)
マグロ *maguro*	tuna
赤身 *akami*	least fatty (and cheapest) piece of tuna
トロ *toro*	fatty part of tuna
鮭 *sake*	salmon
タイ *tai*	sea bream
エビ *ebi*	prawn
イカ *ika*	squid
タコ *tako*	octopus
鯖 *saba*	mackerel

FOOD AND DRINK

アナゴ *anago*	conger eel
鰻 *unagi*	eel
ウニ *uni*	sea urchin
アワビ *awabi*	abalone
牡蠣 *kaki*	oyster
ホタテ貝 *hotate gai*	scallop
たらこ *tarako*	cod roe
いくら *ikura*	salmon roe
めざし *mezashi*	dried sardines
ししゃも *shishamo*	small dried fish
クラゲ *kurage*	jellyfish

◆ Seaweed

Seaweed is a very common food, rich in minerals, and each variety is used in different ways.

のり *nori*	usually used in dried sheets to wrap sushi or shredded on top of rice dishes
わかめ *wakame*	mainly used in miso soup or nabe dishes, or served with *râmen* (Chinese noodles)
昆布 *kombu*	used to make stock, along with bonito fish flakes

◆ Noodles

Noodles made from buckwheat or wheat are very popular, eaten hot or cold according to type and season. **Râmen** come from China, whereas **udon** and **soba** originate in Japan. Each city or region has its own **râmen** speciality

そば *soba*	buckwheat noodles, served hot in broth or chilled on a bamboo tray topped with *nori* seaweed and then dipped in soya sauce
うどん *udon*	thick white wheat noodles, served in broth with meat and vegetables

FOOD AND DRINK

きつねうどん *kitsune udon*	thick white wheat noodles topped with deep-fried sweetened bean curd and spring onions
ラーメン *râmen*	Chinese noodles served in broth
そうめん *sômen*	thin white wheat noodles, served cold in summer
味噌ラーメン *miso râmen*	Chinese noodles in a broth made with fermented soya bean paste *(a speciality of Hokkaidô)*
豚骨ラーメン *tonkotsu râmen*	Chinese noodles in a broth of pork bones *(a speciality of Kyûshû)*
しょう油ラーメン *shôyu râmen*	Chinese noodles in a soya sauce-based broth *(a speciality of the Tokyo area)*
長崎チャンポン *nagasaki champon*	noodles with seafood *(a speciality of the Nagasaki region)*
焼そば *yaki soba*	fried noodles with meat and vegetables and a special sauce
餃子 *gyôza*	Chinese crescent-shaped steamed or fried dumplings containing minced pork, cabbage, spring onions and seasonings, served with a dipping sauce based on soya sauce and vinegar

◆ Okonomiyaki

Okonomiyaki is a speciality of Hiroshima and Osaka, a cross between a large pancake and a pizza, cooked on a hot plate and prepared in slightly different ways in the two cities. In Hiroshima the pancake (batter made from eggs, flour and water) is topped with a variety of chopped cabbage and other vegetables, meat and/or shrimps, often with fried noodles (**yaki soba**) added; an egg is broken on top before the whole thing is turned over to cook the egg. In Osaka the vegetables and meat are mixed into the pancake mixture before cooking. **Okonomiyaki** is served topped with a thick sweet and spicy sauce, dried and powdered **nori** seaweed and **katsuobushi** (dried bonito fish flakes).

◆ Formal seasonal cuisine (kaiseki ryôri)

Kaiseki ryôri is high-class formal seasonal Japanese cuisine which originated in Kyoto. Originally, it was a light meal of two or three vegetarian dishes accompanying the tea ceremony, but over the centuries, it has developed into a meal of many different courses of small dishes, such as raw fish (**sashimi**), **tempura**, grilled fish, vegetables, soup and rice. People go to **kaiseki ryôri** restaurants for special occasions, since the food is time-consuming to prepare and therefore expensive. Some of the most expensive and sought-after dishes are **fugu** (globe-fish), whale, crab, eel and sea urchin. The internal organs of the **fugu** contain a deadly poison, and the fish can only be served at restaurants with specially licensed chefs. It is eaten as **sashimi** or in a **nabe** (stew). Eels are eaten particularly in summer, when they are thought to combat lethargy from the humid heat. They are served sliced and cooked and covered with a sweet sauce in specialized restaurants (**unagiya**).

ウナギ *unagi*	grilled eel
うなぎ屋 *unagiya*	eel restaurant
うな重 *unajû*	eel served on boiled rice on a lacquer tray
ふぐ *fugu*	globe-fish *(also known as blowfish or puffer-fish)*
伊勢エビ *ise ebi*	lobster
カニ *kani*	crab
スッポン *suppon*	softshell turtle
鯨 *kujira*	whale
ナマズ *namazu*	catfish
生き造り *ikizukuri*, 活け造り *ikezukuri*	fish served whole and alive, with slices of flesh having been cut and put back in place

◆ Confectionery, biscuits and crackers

Although Japan does not really have a tradition of desserts, traditional cakes and sweets are called **wagashi**. Elegant small cakes made from rice (**mochi**) and sweetened red bean paste (**anko**) are served at the tea ceremony. There are also many varieties of savoury rice crackers (**sembê**) eaten as snacks.

FOOD AND DRINK

せんべい sembê	savoury rice crackers
もち mochi	sticky rice cakes
あんこ anko	sweetened paste usually made from azuki beans
お汁粉 oshiruko	dessert made from azuki beans in sauce with pieces of sticky rice cake (mochi)
まんじゅう manjû	steamed bun with various fillings, most commonly sweetened azuki bean paste
羊羹 yôkan	sweetened azuki bean jelly

◆ Sweet dishes for summer

カキ氷 kakigôri, フラッペ furappe	shaved ice topped with fruit syrup, sweetened azuki bean paste, green tea or ice cream
ところてん tokoroten	seaweed jelly noodles, eaten with vinegar in the Tokyo region but with sweetened syrup in the Kansai (Osaka/Kyoto/Kobe) region
水羊羹 mizu yôkan	jelly made from seaweed and sweetened azuki beans, less sweet than yôkan

◆ Alcohol

Beer has been popular in Japan since the end of the Second World War. The three main brands are **Asahi**, **Sapporo** and **Kirin**. Rice wine, or **nihonshu**, comes in two varieties: sweet (**amakuchi**) and dry (**karakuchi**). The word **sake** refers to alcohol in general as well as to rice wine, so **nihonshu** is used to make the distinction. There are over 2,500 types available, of varying quality and strength. It can be drunk cold (**hiya**) or hot (**atsukan**), and is always served in tiny cups called **sakazuki**, meaning frequent refills are required! It is not considered polite to pour your own drink when you are in company; if you pour a drink for someone else, he or she will return the favour.

飲み物 nomimono	drink
居酒屋 izakaya	traditional Japanese bar
酒 sake	alcohol; sake, rice wine
日本酒 nihonshu	sake, rice wine
甘口 amakuchi	sweet (sake)

FOOD AND DRINK

辛口 *karakuchi*	dry *(sake)*
あつかん *atsukan*	hot sake
ひや *hiya*	chilled sake
大吟醸酒 *dai ginjô shu*	best quality pure sake made from highly polished rice
焼酎 *shôchû*	clear distilled spirit similar to vodka

◆ Tea

Green tea is a true Japanese speciality. There is an infinite variety available, some of which can cost a fortune. The best tea leaves are protected from the sun as they grow, then carefully harvested and crushed to a powder. At the tea ceremony (**chanoyu** or **sadô**), this powder is stirred into the water with a bamboo whisk called a **chasen** to make a froth. Before drinking, you must turn the tea bowl around in your hands three times in order to admire its beauty. In everyday life, clear green tea is drunk instead of water, and is automatically served in restaurants. Only black tea is served in cafés and tearooms or coffee shops.

緑茶 *ryokucha*	green tea
紅茶 *kôcha*	black tea
ウーロン茶 *ûron cha*	oolong tea *(Chinese)*
玉露 *gyokuro*	high-quality green tea with an intense and slightly sweet taste
抹茶 *matcha*	powdered green tea used in the tea ceremony
煎茶 *sen cha*	most popular variety of clear green tea
茎茶 *kuki cha*	very light green tea from tea stalks
ほうじ茶 *hôji cha*	roasted green tea
玄米茶 *gemmai cha*	green tea mixed with roasted brown rice
麦茶 *mugi cha*	barley tea *(served chilled in summer)*

GOING OUT

The free English-language magazine **Metropolitan** provides information about the films and plays showing in Tokyo, and comes out every Friday. It can be found in large record shops like **Tower Records** and **HMV**, or in some bars.

Going to the cinema is very expensive, and hence not as common as in Europe. A more popular activity is **karaoke**: in Japan, this often takes place in small booths where people meet for a drink and a chat, and sing for their friends. The repertoire includes **J-Pop** (Japanese pop music) as well as English-language songs.

If you get the chance, go and watch one of the forms of ancient Japanese theatre, **noh** and **kabuki**.

Japanese people tend to socialize by going out, and rarely entertain at home. However, if you are invited to someone's house, remember to bring a little present, be on time and be sure to take off your shoes in the entrance as soon as you go in! You will be given slippers to wear in the house, but these too should be removed before walking on **tatami** mats.

The basics

ballet	バレエ *barê*
band	バンド *bando*
bar	バー *bâ*, スナック *sunakku (a "bâ" has hostesses and can be very expensive*
cinema	映画館 *êgakan*
circus	サーカス *sâkasu*
classical music	クラシック *kurashikku*
club	クラブ *kurabu (most Japanese clubs are slightly more sophisticated hostess bars)*
concert	コンサート *konsâto*
dubbed film	吹き替えされた映画 *fukikaesareta êga*
festival	祭り *matsuri*, フェスティバル *fesutibaru*

film	映画 *êga*
group	団体 *dantai*, グループ *gurûpu*
jazz	ジャズ *jazu*
modern dance	モダンダンス *modan dansu*
musical	ミュージカル *myûjikaru*
party	パーティー *pâtî*
play	芝居 *shibai*, 劇 *geki*
pop music	ポップス *poppusu*
rock music	ロック *rokku*
show	ショー *shô*
subtitled film	字幕付き映画 *jimaku tsuki êga*
theatre	劇場 *gekijo*
ticket	チケット *chiketto*, 切符 *kippu*
to book	予約する *yoyaku suru*
to go out	出かける *dekakeru*

SUGGESTIONS AND INVITATIONS

Expressing yourself

where can we go?
どこへ行きましょうか。
doko e ikimashô ka?

what do you want to do?
何がしたいですか。
nani ga shitai desu ka?

shall we go for a drink?
飲みに行きましょうか。
nomi ni ikimashô ka?

what are you doing tonight?
今夜、何をしますか。
kon'ya, nani o shimasu ka?

do you have plans?
何か予定がありますか。
nani ka yotê ga arimasu ka?

would you like to …?
… たいですか。
… tai desu ka?

would you like to go to …?
… へ行きませんか。
… e ikimasen ka?

we were thinking of going to …
… へ行こうと思っています。
… e ikô to omotte imasu

I can't today, but maybe some other time
今日はだめですが、また別の日に。
kyô wa dame desu ga, mata betsu no hi ni

GOING OUT

71

I'm not sure I can make it
行けるかどうかちょっとわかりません。
ikeru ka dô ka chotto wakarimasen

I'd love to
喜んで。
yorokonde

ARRANGING TO MEET

Expressing yourself

what time shall we meet?
何時に会いましょうか。
nan ji ni aimashô ka?

where shall we meet?
どこで会いましょうか。
doko de aimashô ka?

would it be possible to meet a bit later?
もう少し遅くに会えますか。
mô sukoshi osoku ni aemasu ka?

I have to meet … at nine
… と9時に会わなければなりません。
… to ku ji ni awanakereba narimasen

I don't know where it is but I'll find it on the map
それがどこか知りませんが、地図で調べます。
sore ga doko ka shirimasen ga, chizu de shirabemasu

see you tomorrow night
では、また明日の晩。
de wa, mata ashita no ban

I'll meet you later, I have to stop by the hotel first
では、また後で。まずホテルに寄らなければなりません。
de wa, mata ato de. mazu hoteru ni yoranakereba narimasen

I'll call/text you if there's a change of plan
もし変更があれば、電話・テキストします。
moshi henkô ga areba, denwa/tekisuto shimasu

are you going to eat beforehand?
前もって食事をしますか。
mae motte shokuji o shimasu ka?

sorry I'm late
遅くなってすみません。
osoku natte sumimasen

Understanding

それでいいですか。
sore de î desu ka?
is that OK with you?

8時頃、迎えに行きます。
hachi ji goro mukae ni ikimasu
I'll come and pick you up about 8

そこで会いましょう。
soko de aimashô
I'll meet you there

… の外で会いましょう。
… no soto de aimashô
we can meet outside …

電話番号を教えますから、明日電話してください。
denwa bangô o oshiemasu kara, ashita denwa shite kudasai
I'll give you my number and you can call me tomorrow

FILMS, SHOWS AND CONCERTS

Expressing yourself

is there a guide to what's on?
劇や映画の情報を載せたイベント情報誌はありますか。
geki ya êga no jôhô o noseta ibento jôhôshi wa arimasu ka?

I'd like three tickets for …
… のチケットを3枚ください。
… no chiketto o sam mai kudasai

two tickets, please
チケット2枚、お願いします。
chiketto ni mai onegai shimasu

it's called …
… という名前です。
… to yû namae desu

I've seen the trailer
予告編を見ました。
yokokuhen o mimashita

what time does it start?
何時に始まりますか。
nan ji ni hajimarimasu ka?

I'd like to go and see a show
ショーを見に行きたいと思います。
shô o mi ni ikitai to omoimasu

I'll find out whether there are still tickets available
まだチケットがあるか調べてみます。
mada chiketto ga aru ka shirabete mimasu

do we need to book in advance?
前もって予約が必要ですか。
mae motte yoyaku ga hitsuyô desu ka?

how long is it on for?
いつまでやっていますか。
itsu made yatte imasu ka?

are there tickets for another day?
別の日のチケットはありますか。
betsu no hi no chiketto wa arimasu ka?

I'd like to go to a bar with some live music
生演奏をやっているバーに行きたいと思います。
nama ensô o yatte iru bâ ni ikitai to omoimasu

are there any free concerts?
無料のコンサートをどこかでやっていますか。
muryô no konsâto o doko ka de yatte imasu ka?

what sort of music is it?
どんな音楽ですか。
donna ongaku desu ka?

Understanding

大ヒット作 *dai hitto saku*	blockbuster
予約 *yoyaku*	bookings
切符売場 *kippu uriba*	box office
昼興行 *hiru kôgyô*, マチネ *machine*	matinée
… から一般公開 … *kara ippan kôkai*	on general release from …
日本の伝統音楽 *nihon no dentô ongaku*	traditional Japanese music

野外コンサートです。
yagai konsâto desu
it's an open-air concert

来週、公開です。
raishû kôkai desu
it comes out next week

その上演は売り切れです。
sono jôen wa urikire desu
that showing's sold out

批評ではほめられていました。
hihyô de wa homerarete imashita
it's had very good reviews

オデオンで午後8時からです。
odeon de gogo hachi ji kara desu
it's on at 8pm at the Odeon

… まで全部売り切れています。
… made zembu urikirete imasu
it's all booked up until …

前もって予約する必要はありません。
mae motte yoyaku suru hitsuyô wa arimasen
there's no need to book in advance

その劇は、休憩も含めて。一時間半です。
sono geki wa kyûkê mo fukumete ichi jikan han desu
the play lasts an hour and a half, including the interval

携帯電話の電源をお切りください。
kêtai denwa no dengen o okiri kudasai
please turn off your mobile phones

PARTIES AND CLUBS

Expressing yourself

I'm having a little leaving party tonight
今夜、ちょっとしたお別れパーティーをします。
kon ya, chotto shita owakare patî o shimasu

should I bring something to drink?
何か飲み物を持って行きましょうか。
nani ka nomimono o motte ikimashô ka?

we could go to a club afterwards
その後でクラブに行ってもいいでしょう。
sono ato de kurabu ni itte mo î deshô

do you have to pay to get in?
入場は有料ですか。
nyûjô wa yûryô desu ka?

I have to meet someone inside
中にいる人とちょっと会いたいんですが。
naka ni iru hito to chotto aitai n desu ga

the DJ's really cool
あのＤＪ、すごくカッコいい。
ano DJ sugoku kakko î

can I buy you a drink?
飲み物をおごらせてください。
nomimono o ogorasete kudasai

thanks, but I'm with my boyfriend
ありがとう。でもボーイフレンドと来ています。
arigatô. demo bôifurendo to kite imasu

no thanks, I don't smoke
いいえ、結構です。タバコは吸いません.
îe, kekkô desu. tabako wa suimasen

Understanding

携帯品一時預かり所 *kêtaihin ichiji azukarijo*	cloakroom
無料ドリンク *muryô dorinku*	free drink
夜12時過ぎは1000円 *yoru jûni ji sugi wa sen en*	1000 yen after midnight

踊りませんか。
odorimasen ka?
do you want to dance?

一緒に飲みませんか。
issho ni nomimasen ka?
shall we have a drink together?

マッチかライター、持っています。
matchi ka raitâ motte imasu ka?
have you got a light?

タバコ、あります。
tabako arimasu?
have you got a cigarette?

また会えますか。
mata aemasu ka?
can we see each other again?

家まで送りましょうか。
ie made okurimashô ka?
can I see you home?

TOURISM AND SIGHTSEEING

Tourist information offices are often close to or inside railway stations, and are open daily from 10am to 5pm. Make sure you pick up plenty of leaflets and a streetmap, as there are few maps on display in towns. If you do get lost, you can buy a map in a **kombini** (see p. 90). Most places of interest do not offer guided tours; instead, visitors can generally hire headsets with commentary in Japanese or English. There is usually an entrance fee, and flash photography is forbidden (フラッシュ禁止 *furasshu kinshi*) in many temples and museums. You may need to take your shoes off to go inside temples and shrines.

The basics

ancient	古代の *kodai no*
antique	(adj) 古風な *kofû na*; (n) 骨董品 *kottôhin*, アンティーク *antîku*
area	地域 *chi-iki*
castle	（お）城 *(o)shiro*
century	世紀 *sêki*
church	教会 *kyôkai*
exhibition	展覧会 *tenrankai*
gallery	美術館 *bijutsukan*
modern art	近代美術 *kindai bijutsu*
mosque	モスク *mosuku*
museum	博物館 *hakubutsukan*
painting	絵 *e*, 絵画 *kaiga*
park	公園 *kôen*
ruins	廃墟 *haikyo*
sculpture	彫刻 *chôkoku*
shrine	神社 *jinja*
statue	像 *zô*
streetmap	ストリートマップ *sutorîto mappu*

synagogue	シナゴーグ *shinagôgu*
temple	(お)寺 *(o)tera*
tour guide	観光ガイド *kankô gaido*
tourist	観光客 *kankôkyaku*
tourist information centre	観光案内所 *kankô annaijo*
town centre	中心街 *chûshingai*

Expressing yourself

I'd like some information on …
… についての情報がほしいんですが。
… ni tsuite no jôhô ga hoshî n desu ga

can you tell me where the tourist information centre is?
どこに観光案内所があるか教えてくれませんか。
doko ni kankô annaijo ga aru ka oshiete kuremasen ka?

do you have a streetmap of the town?
この街のストリートマップはありますか。
kono machi no sutorîto mappu wa arimasu ka?

I was told there's an old temple you can visit
古いお寺があると聞きました。
furui otera ga aru to kikimashita

can you show me where it is on the map?
どこにあるか、この地図で教えてくれませんか。
doko ni aru ka, kono chizu de oshiete kuremasen ka?

how do you get there?
どうやってそこに行ったらいいですか。
dô yatte soko ni ittara î desu ka?

is it free?
無料ですか。
muryô desu ka?

when was it built?
いつ建てられましたか。
itsu tateraremashita ka?

Understanding

入場無料 *nyûjô muryô*		admission free
閉館 *hêkan*		closed
戦争 *sensô*		war
いくさ *ikusa*		war
侵略 *shinryaku*		invasion
中世 *chûsê*		medieval
開館 *kaikan*		open
中国 *chûgoku*		China
韓国 *kankoku*		Korea
改装 *kaisô*		renovation
修復工事 *shûfuku kôji*		restoration work
城下町 *jôkamachi*		castle town
ガイド付き見学コース		guided tour
gaido tsuki kengaku kôsu		
現在位置 *genzai ichi*		you are here *(on a map)*

着いてから聞いてみてください。
tsuite kara kîte mite kudasai
you'll have to ask when you get there

次のガイド付き見学コースは2時からです。
tsugi no gaido tsuki kengaku kôsu wa ni ji kara desu
the next guided tour starts at 2 o'clock

MUSEUMS, EXHIBITIONS AND MONUMENTS

Expressing yourself

I've heard there's a very good ... exhibition on at the moment
今、すばらしい ... の展覧会をやっていると聞きました。
ima subarashî ... no tenrankai o yatte iru to kikimashita

how much is it to get in?
入るのにいくら掛かりますか。
hairu no ni ikura kakarimasu ka?

is this ticket valid for the exhibition as well?
このチケットで展覧会も入場できますか。
kono chiketto de tenrankai mo nyûjô dekimasu ka?

are there any discounts for young people?
学生割引はありますか。
gakusê waribiki wa arimasu ka?

is it open on Sundays?
日曜日も開いていますか。
nichiyôbi mo aite imasu ka?

two adults and one child, please
大人2枚と子供1枚、お願いします。
otona ni mai to kodomo ichi mai onegai shimasu

I have a student card
学生証を持っています。
gakusê shô o motte imasu

Understanding

オーディオガイド *ôdiogaido*	audioguide
チケット *chiketto*, 切符 *kippu*	ticket
切符売り場 *kippu uriba*	ticket office
特別展 *tokubetsu ten*	temporary exhibition
常設展 *jôsetsu ten*	permanent exhibition
フラッシュ禁止 *furasshu kinshi*	no flash photography
撮影禁止 *satsuê kinshi*	no photography
順路 *junro*	this way
お静かに願います *oshizuka ni negaimasu*	silence, please
触らないでください *sawaranaide kudasai*	please do not touch

博物館の入場料は … です。
hakubutsukan no nyûjô ryô wa … desu
admission to the museum costs …

このチケット・切符で展覧会もご覧いただけます。
kono chiketto/kippu de tenrankai mo goran itadakemasu
this ticket also allows you access to the exhibition

学生証をお持ちですか。
gakusê shô o omochi desu ka?
do you have your student card?

GIVING YOUR IMPRESSIONS

Expressing yourself

it's beautiful
きれいです。
kirê desu

it was beautiful
きれいでした。
kirê deshita

it's fantastic
すばらしいです。
subarashî desu

it was fantastic
すばらしかったです。
subarashikatta desu

I really enjoyed it
とてもよかったです。
totemo yokatta desu

I didn't like it that much
そんなに面白くありませんでした。
sonna ni omoshiroku arimasen deshita

it was a bit boring
ちょっとつまらなかったです。
chotto tsumaranakatta desu

I'm not really a fan of modern art
近代美術はあまり好きじゃありません。
kindai bijutsu wa amari suki ja arimasen

it's expensive for what it is
内容の割には高いです。
naiyô no wari ni wa takai desu

it's very touristy
とても観光地化しています。
totemo kankôchika shite imasu

it was really crowded
とても混んでいました。
totemo konde imashita

we didn't go in the end, the queue was too long
行列が長かったので、結局行きませんでした。
gyôretsu ga nagakatta node, kekkyoku ikimasen deshita

we didn't have time to see everything
全部見る時間はありませんでした。
zembu miru jikan wa arimasen deshita

Understanding

有名な *yûmê na*	famous
絵のように美しい *e no yô ni utsukushî*	picturesque
典型的な *tenkêteki na*	typical
伝統的な *dentôteki na*	traditional

… を絶対、見ないといけません。
… o zettai minai to ikemasen
you really must go and see …

… に行くのをお勧めします。
… ni iku no o osusume shimasu
I recommend going to …

町全体のすばらしい景色が見られます。
machi zentai no subarashî keshiki ga miraremasu
there's a wonderful view over the whole city

ちょっと観光地化しすぎました。
chotto kankôchika shisugimashita
it's become a bit too touristy

SPORTS AND GAMES

The most popular sports in Japan are baseball, sumo wrestling, football and golf. There are 12 professional baseball teams, the favourites being the **Yomiuri Giants** (Tokyo), the **Chûnichi Dragons** (Nagoya) and the **Hanshin Tigers** (Osaka).

For information on walks and hiking, ask at the area's tourist information office (観光案内所 *kankô annai jo*) or at hotel reception desks.

In winter, you can ski in Koshin-etsu, Tôhoku and Hokkaidô – some pistes are open day and night. Chiba has an indoor ski centre, where artificial snow means guaranteed conditions all year round.

Traditional Japanese games include **shôgi** (similar to chess), **igo** (go), **koma** (a game played with wooden spinning tops) and **tako** (kite-flying). **Sugoroku** (similar to snakes and ladders) and Othello are also popular.

The basics

ball	ボール *bôru*
baseball	野球 *yakyû*
basketball	バスケット *basuketto*
bicycle	自転車 *jitensha*
board game	ボードゲーム *bôdo gêmu*
cards	トランプ *torampu*
chess	チェス *chesu*
country(side)	田舎 *inaka*
cross-country skiing	クロスカントリースキー *kurosukantorî sukî*
cycling	サイクリング *saikuringu*
downhill skiing	滑降スキー *kakkô sukî*
football	サッカー *sakkâ*
golf	ゴルフ *gorufu*
hiking path	ハイキングコース *haikingu kôsu*, 遊歩道 *yuhodô*
match	試合 *shiai*

mountain biking	マウンテンバイク *maunten baiku*
pool (game)	玉突き *tamatsuki*
rugby	ラグビー *ragubî*
ski	スキー *sukî*
snowboarding	スノーボード *sunôbôdo*
sport	スポーツ *supôtsu*
sumo wrestling	相撲 *sumô*
surfing	サーフィン *sâfin*
swimming	水泳 *suiê*
swimming pool	プール *pûru*
tennis	テニス *tenisu*
trip	旅行 *ryokô*
walk	散歩 *sampo*
to go for a walk	散歩する *sampo suru*
to go hiking	ハイキングをする *haikingu o suru*
to have a game of ...	... の試合をする *... no shiai o suru*
to play ...	... をする *... o suru*

Expressing yourself

I'd like to hire ... for an hour
... を1時間、借りたいんですが。
... o ichi jikan karitai n desu ga

are there ... lessons available?
... のレッスンはありますか。
... no ressun wa arimasu ka?

how much is it per person per hour?
1人1時間いくらですか。
hitori ichi jikan ikura desu ka?

I'm not very sporty
運動神経がいいほうじゃありません。
undô shinkê ga î hô ja arimasen

I've never done it before
一度もやったことがありません。
ichi do mo yatta koto ga arimasen

I've done it once or twice, a long time ago
ずいぶん昔に1, 2回やったことがあります。
zuibun mukashi ni ichi, ni kai yatta koto ga arimasu

I'm exhausted!
くたくたです。
kutakuta desu

I'd like to go and watch a football match/sumo match
サッカーの試合・相撲を見に行きたいと思います。
sakkâ no shiai/sumô o mi ni ikitai to omoimasu

shall we stop for a picnic?
ちょっと休んで、お弁当にしましょうか。
chotto yasunde, obentô ni shimashô ka?

we played ...
... をしました。
... o shimashita

Understanding

... レンタル ... *rentaru*   ... for hire

経験がありますか、まったくの初心者ですか。
kêken ga arimasu ka, mattaku no shoshinsha desu ka?
do you have any experience, or are you a complete beginner?

... の保証金が必要です。
... no hoshôkin ga hitsuyô desu
there is a deposit of ...

保険は強制で、金額は ... です。
hoken wa kyôsê de, kingaku wa ... desu
insurance is compulsory and costs ...

HIKING

Expressing yourself

are there any hiking paths around here?
この辺にハイキングコース・遊歩道はありますか。
kono hen ni haikingu kôsu/yuhodô wa arimasu ka?

can you recommend any good walks in the area?
この辺で歩くのにいいところを教えてくれませんか。
kono hen de aruku no ni î tokoro o oshiete kuremasen ka?

I've heard there's a nice walk by the lake
湖の近くに歩くのにいい所があると聞きました。
mizu-umi no chikaku ni aruku no ni î tokoro ga aru to kikimashita

we're looking for a short walk somewhere round here
この辺りで散歩できるところを探しています。
kono atari de sampo dekiru tokoro o sagashite imasu

can I hire hiking boots?
ハイキングブーツを借りられますか。
haikingu bûtsu o kariraremasu ka?

how long does the hike take?
ハイキングはどれくらいかかりますか。
haikingu wa dore kurai kakarimasu ka?

is it very steep?
きついですか。
kitsui desu ka?

where's the start of the path?
どこが遊歩道の始まりですか。
doko ga yuhodô no hajimari desu ka?

is the path waymarked?
遊歩道には標識がありますか。
yuhodô ni wa hyôshiki ga arimasu ka?

is it a circular path?
一周して戻って来る道ですか。
isshû shite modotte kuru michi desu ka?

Understanding

平均所要時間 *hêkin shoyô jikan*   average duration *(of walk)*

休憩も含めて大体3時間です。
kyûkê mo fukumete daitai san jikan desu
it's about three hours' walk including rest stops

防水の上着とウォーキングシューズを持ってきてください。
bôsui no uwagi to wôkingu shûzu o motte kite kudasai
bring a waterproof jacket and some walking shoes

SKIING AND SNOWBOARDING

Expressing yourself

I'd like to hire skis, poles and boots
スキー板とストックとブーツを借りたいんですが。
sukî ita to sutokku to bûtsu o karitai n desu ga

I'd like to hire a snowboard
スノーボードを借りたいんですが。
sunôbôdo o karitai n desu ga

they're too big/small
大きすぎます・小さすぎます。
ôkisugimasu/chîsasugimasu

a day pass
一日券
ichi nichi ken

I'm a complete beginner
全く初めてです。
mattaku hajimete desu

Understanding

リフト *rifuto*   chair lift
リフト券 *rifuto ken*   lift pass
スキーリフト *sukî rifuto* ski lift

Tバーリフト *tî bâ rifuto*   T-bar, button lift

OTHER SPORTS

Expressing yourself

where can we hire bikes?
どこで自転車を借りられますか。
doko de jitensha o kariraremasu ka?

are there any cycle paths?
サイクリングコースはありますか。
saikuringu kôsu wa arimasu ka?

does anyone have a football?
誰かサッカーボールを持っていますか。
dare ka sakkâ bôru o motte imasu ka?

which team do you support?   **I support ...**
どのチームのファンですか。   ... のファンです。
dono chîmu no fan desu ka?   *... no fan desu*

is there an open-air swimming pool?
屋外プールはありますか。
okugai pûru wa arimasu ka?

I've never been diving before
ダイビングは初めてです。
daibingu wa hajimete desu

I'd like to take beginners' sailing lessons
初心者用のヨットコースに入りたいんですが。
shoshinsha yô no yotto kôsu ni hairitai n desu ga

Understanding

駅から遠くないところに公営のテニスコートがあります。
eki kara tôkunai tokoro ni kôê no tenisu kôto ga arimasu
there's a public tennis court not far from the station

テニスコートは空いていません。
tenisu kôto wa aite imasen
the tennis court's occupied

乗馬は初めてですか。
jôba wa hajimete desu ka?
is this the first time you've been horse-riding?

泳げますか。
oyogemasu ka?
can you swim?

バスケットはしますか。
basuketto wa shimasu ka?
do you play basketball?

INDOOR GAMES

Expressing yourself

shall we have a game of cards?
トランプをしましょうか。
torampu o shimashô ka?

does anyone know any good card games?
誰か面白いトランプを知っていますか。
dare ka omoshiroi torampu o shitte imasu ka?

it's your turn
そちらの番です。
sochira no ban desu

Understanding

マージャンはできますか。
mâjan wa dekimasu ka?
do you know how to play mah jong?

トランプを持っていますか。
torampu o motte imasu ka?
do you have a pack of cards?

Some informal expressions

へとへとです。　*hetoheto desu* I'm absolutely knackered
彼には手も足も出なかった。　*kare ni wa te mo ashi mo denakatta*
he totally thrashed me

SHOPPING

Kombini, or convenience stores, are small local shops open 24 hours a day. They sell food, toiletries, stationery and other essential items. The biggest chains are **Seven/Eleven**, **Lawson**, **Family Mart** and **am/pm**. You can usually find small shops and minimarkets near railway stations but they will often be closed on Sundays. Big supermarkets and hypermarkets such as **Jusco**, **Ito Yokado** and **Seiyu** are open daily, including Sundays. You can also buy a vast range of items from vending machines (**jidôhambaiki**).

Department stores (such as **Isetan**, **Mitsukoshi**, **Takashimaya**, **Seibu** and **Odakyu**) are the place to go for high-quality goods; they are generally closed on Wenesdays.

Almost all signs have a transcription in roman letters, and prices are always written in arabic numerals. Clothes sizes are smaller than you will be used to at home: a Small in Japan would be an Extra Small in the West, and so on. Shoe sizes are given in centimetres. Most transactions are made in cash.

The basics

bakery	パン屋 *pan ya*
bookshop	本屋 *hon ya*
butcher's	肉屋 *niku ya*
cash desk	レジ *reji*
cheap	安い *yasui*
checkout	精算 *sêsan*
cigarettes	タバコ *tabako*
clothes	服 *fuku*
convenience store	コンビニ *kombini*
cost	値段 *nedan*
department store	デパート *depâto*
dictionary	辞書 *jisho*
expensive	高い *takai*
gram	グラム *guramu*
greengrocer's	八百屋 *yao ya*

kilo	キロ *kiro*
matches	マッチ *matchi*
present	プレゼント *purezento*, 贈り物 *okurimono*
price	値段 *nedan*
receipt	レシート *reshîto*, 領収書 *ryôshûsho*
refund	払い戻し *haraimodoshi*
sales	セール *sêru*
sales assistant	店員 *ten'in*
sales tax	消費税 *shôhizê*
shop	店 *mise*
shopping arcade	商店街 *shôtengai*
shopping centre	ショッピングセンター *shoppingu sentâ*, モール *môru*
souvenir	お土産 *omiyage*
supermarket	スーパー *sûpâ*
tissues	ティッシュ（ペーパー）*tisshu(pêpâ)*
umbrella	傘 *kasa*
vending machine	自動販売機 *jidôhambaiki*
to buy	買う *kau*
to cost	かかる *kakaru*
to pay	払う *harau*
to sell	売る *uru*

Expressing yourself

is there a supermarket near here?
この近くにスーパーはありますか。
kono chikaku ni sûpâ wa arimasu ka?

where can I buy cigarettes?
どこでタバコは買えますか。
doko de tabako wa kaemasu ka?

I'd like …
… をください。
… o kudasai

I'm looking for …
… を探しています。
… o sagashite imasu

do you sell ...?
... はありますか。
... wa arimasu ka?

do you know where I might find some ...?
どこで ... が買えるか知っていますか。
doko de ... ga kaeru ka shitte imasu ka?

can you order it for me?
それを注文してくれますか。
sore o chûmon shite kuremasu ka?

how much is this?
これはいくらですか。
kore wa ikura desu ka?

I'll take it
それにします。
sore ni shimasu

I haven't got much money
あまりお金がありません。
amari okane ga arimasen

I haven't got enough money
そんなにお金を持っていません。
sonna ni okane o motte imasen

that's everything, thanks
それだけです。ありがとう。
sore dake desu. arigatô

I think you've made a mistake with my change
お釣りが間違ってるんじゃないかと思うんですが。
otsuri ga machigatte ru n ja nai ka to omou n desu ga

Understanding

（英字）新聞 (êji) shimbun	(English language) newspaper
朝市 asa ichi	(morning) market
... 時から ... 時まで営業 ... ji kara ... ji made êgyô	open from ... to ...
特別奉仕 tokubetsu hôshi	special offer
セール sêru	sales

何か他にお入用ですか。
nani ka hoka ni o iriyô desu ka?
will there be anything else?

リボンをおかけしましょうか。
ribon o okake shimashô ka?
shall I put a ribbon on it?

PAYING

Expressing yourself

where do I pay?
どこで払ったらいいですか。
doko de harattara î desu ka?

how much do I owe you?
おいくらですか。
oikura desu ka?

could you write it down for me, please?
書いてくれますか。
kaite kuremasu ka?

can I pay by credit card?
クレジットカードは使えますか。
kurejitto kâdo wa tsukaemasu ka?

I'll pay in cash
現金で払います。
genkin de haraimasu

I'm sorry, I haven't got any change
すみません、小銭がありません。
sumimasen, kozen ga arimasen.

please could you give me change for this?
小銭に両替してもらえますか。
kozeni ni ryôgae shite moraemasu ka?

can I have a receipt?
レシート・領収書をください。
reshîto/ryôshûsho o kudasai

Understanding

レジでお支払いください。
reji de oshiharai kudasai
pay at the cash desk

何でお支払いになりますか。
nan de oshiharai ni narimasu ka?
how would you like to pay?

細かいのをお持ちですか。
komakai no o omochi desu ka?
do you have anything smaller?

身分証明書をお持ちですか。
mibunshômêsho o omochi desu ka?
have you got any ID?

ここに署名・サインをお願いします。
koko ni shomê/sain o onegai shimasu
could you sign here, please?

FOOD

Expressing yourself

where can I buy food around here?
この辺で食べ物を買えるのはどこですか。
kono hen de tabemono o kaeru no wa doko desu ka?

is there a bakery around here?
この近くにパン屋はありますか。
kono chikaku ni pan ya wa arimasu ka?

I'm looking for the cereal aisle
シリアルはどこにありますか。
shiriaru wa doko ni arimasu ka?

two slices of breaded pork cutlet, please
トンカツを二枚ください。
tonkatsu o ni mai kudasai

one pack of sushi, please
すしを 1 パックください。
sushi o hito pakku kudasai

it's for four people
4人分です。
yo nin bun desu

about 300 grams
300グラムくらい。
sambyaku guramu kurai

five apples, please
りんごを5個、お願いします。
ringo o go ko onegai shimasu

a bit less/more
もう少し少なく・多く。
mô sukoshi sukunaku/ôku

can I taste it?
試食してもいいですか。
shishoku shite mo î desu ka?

does it travel well?
日持ちしますか。
himochi shimasu ka?

Understanding

賞味期限 *shômi kigen*	best before
デリカテッセン *derikatessen*	delicatessen
自家製 *jika sê*	homemade
地方の特産品 *chihô no tokusanhin*	local specialities
無農薬 *munôyaku*	organic

朝市は毎朝10時までやっています。
asa ichi wa mai asa jû ji made yatte imasu
there's a market every morning until 10am

その角に遅くまでやっているコンビニがあります。
sono kado ni osoku made yatte iru kombini ga arimasu
there's a convenience store just on the corner that's open late

CLOTHES

Colours	
red	赤 *aka*
blue	青 *ao*
green	緑 *midori*
yellow	黄色 *kîro*
white	白 *shiro*
black	黒 *kuro*
pink	ピンク *pinku*
grey	グレイ *gurê*
brown	茶色 *chairo*

Expressing yourself

I'm looking for the menswear section
紳士服売り場を探しています。
shinshi fuku uriba o sagashite imasu

no thanks, I'm just looking
いいえ、結構です。見ているだけです。
îe, kekkô desu. mite iru dake desu

can I try it on?
試着してもいいですか。
shichaku shite mo î desu ka?

I'd like to try the one in the window
ショーウィンドウにあるのを試着してみたいんですが。
shôwindô ni aru no o shichaku shite mitai n desu ga

where are the changing rooms?
試着室はどこですか。
shichaku shitsu wa doko desu ka?

it doesn't fit
サイズが合いません。
saizu ga aimasen

it's too big/small
大きすぎます・小さすぎます。
ôkisugimasu/chîsasugimasu

do you have it in another colour?
他の色はありませんか。
hoka no iro wa arimasen ka?

do you have it in a smaller/bigger size?
もっと小さい・大きいサイズはありませんか。
motto chîsai/ôkî saizu wa arimasen ka?

do you have them in red?
これの赤はありませんか。
kore no aka wa arimasen ka?

yes, that's fine, I'll take them
ええ、これでいいです。これにします。
ê, kore de î desu. kore ni shimasu

no, I don't like it
いいえ、あまり好きじゃないです。
îe, amari suki ja nai desu

I'll think about it
考えてみます。
kangaete mimasu

I'd like to return this, it doesn't fit
これを返品したいんですが。サイズが合いませんでした。
kore o hempin shitai n desu ga. saizu ga aimasen deshita

this ... has a hole in it, can I get a refund?
この … は穴が開いています。返金してもらえますか。
kono … wa ana ga aite imasu. henkin shite moraemasu ka?

Understanding

試着室 *shichaku shitsu*	changing rooms
子供服 *kodomo fuku*	children's clothes
婦人服 *fujin fuku*	ladieswear
下着・ランジェリー *shitagi/ranjerî*	lingerie
紳士服 *shinshi fuku*	menswear
日曜営業 *nichiyôbi êgyô*	open Sunday
セール商品は返品できません *sêru shôhin wa hempin dekimasen*	sale items cannot be returned

いらっしゃいませ。何にいたしましょう。
irasshaimase. nan ni itashimashô?
hello, can I help you?

青と黒しかございません。
ao to kuro shika gozaimasen
we only have it in blue or black

そのサイズは品切れでございます。
sono saizu wa shinagire de gozaimasu
we don't have any left in that size

よくお似合いです。
yoku oniai desu
it suits you

ぴったりです。
pittari desu
it's a good fit

もし合わなければ、返品していただけます。
moshi awanakereba, hempin shite itadakemasu
you can bring it back if it doesn't fit

SOUVENIRS AND PRESENTS

Expressing yourself

I'm looking for a present to take home
家への土産を探しています。
ie e no miyage o sagashite imasu

I'd like something that's easy to transport
持ち運びしやすいものが何かほしいです。
mochihakobi shiyasui mono ga nani ka hoshî desu

it's for a little girl of four
4歳の女の子用です。
yon sai no onna no ko yô desu

could you gift-wrap it for me?
プレゼント用に包んでくれますか。
purezento yô ni tsutsunde kuremasu ka?

Understanding

人形 *ningyô*	doll
扇子 *sensu*	fan
民芸品 *mingêhin*	folk crafts
手作り *tezukuri*	handmade
和紙 *washi*	Japanese paper
漆器 *shikki*	lacquerware
木製品・銀製品・金製品・ウール製品 *moku sêhin/gin sêhin/kin sêhin/ûru sêhin*	made of wood/silver/gold/wool
陶器 *tôki*	pottery
伝統工芸品 *dentô kôgêhin*	traditionally made product
木版画 *mokuhanga*	woodblock prints
風呂敷 *furoshiki*	wrapping cloth

ご予算はどのくらいですか。
goyosan wa dono kurai desu ka?
how much do you want to spend?

プレゼントですか。
purezento desu ka?
is it for a present?

この地方独特のものです。
kono chihô dokutoku no mono desu
it's typical of the region

Some informal expressions

ぼったくりだ *bottakuri da* that's a rip-off!
文無しです *mon nashi desu* I'm skint
目玉が飛び出すほど高い *medama ga tobidasu hodo takai*
it costs an arm and a leg
掘り出し物です *horidashimono desu* it's a real bargain
大幅値下げ *ôhaba nesage* prices slashed

SHOPPING

99

PHOTOS

(i)

The Japanese have long had a passion for photography. Discount stores such as **Bic Camera**, **Yodobashi Camera** and **Sakuraya** all offer a huge choice, whether you're looking for a cheap disposable camera or the most cutting-edge telephoto lens, a digital camera or an underwater camera. There are whole areas that sell nothing but electronics, such as Akihabara in Tokyo and Nihonbashi in Osaka. If you do buy any electronic appliances in Japan, make sure they will be compatible when you take them home.

Having photos developed is fairly cheap in Japan, whether in specialist shops, supermarkets or **kombini** (see p. 90). The standard format is 8.8 cm by 12.6 cm.

The basics

battery	電池 *denchi*
black and white	白黒 *shiro kuro*
camera	カメラ *kamera*
colour	カラー *karâ*
copy	焼き増し *yakimashi*
digital camera	デジタルカメラ *dejitaru kamera*, デジカメ *dejikame*
disposable camera	使い捨てカメラ *tsukaisute kamera*
enlargement	引き伸ばし *hikonobashi*
film	フイルム *fuirumu*, フィルム *firumu*
flash	フラッシュ *furasshu*
glossy	光沢 *kôtaku*
matt	光沢なし *kôtaku nashi*
memory card	メモリーカード *memorî kâdo*
negative	ネガ *nega*
passport photo	パスポート写真 *pasupôto shashin*
photo booth	3分間写真 *sam pun kan shashin*
reprint	焼き増し *yakimashi*
slide	スライド *suraido*

| to get photos developed | 写真を現像してもらう *shashin o genzô shite morau* |
| to take a photo/photos | 写真を撮る *shashin o toru* |

Expressing yourself

could you take a photo of us, please?
写真を撮ってもらえますか。
shashin o totte moraemasu ka?

you just have to press this button
このボタンを押すだけです。
kono botan o osu dake desu

I'd like a 200 ASA colour film
アーサー200のカラーフィルムをください。
âsâ nihyaku no karâ firumu o kudasai

do you have black and white films?
白黒のフィルムはありますか。
shiro kuro no firumu wa arimasu ka?

how much is it to develop a film of 36 photos?
36枚撮りの現像はいくらですか。
sanjûroku mai dori no genzô wa ikura desu ka?

I'd like to have this film developed
このフィルムを現像してください。
kono firumu o genzô shite kudasai

I'd like extra copies of some of the photos
焼き増ししてほしいものがあります。
yakimashi shite hoshî mono ga arimasu

three copies of this one and two of this one
これを3枚、これを2枚焼き増ししてください。
kore o sam mai, kore o ni mai yakimashi shite kudasai

can I print my digital photos here?
ここでデジタルカメラの印刷はできますか。
koko de dejitaru kamera no insatsu wa dekimasu ka?

can you put these photos on a CD for me?
この写真をCDに入れてくれますか。
kono shashin o shîdî ni irete kuremasu ka?

I've come to pick up my photos
写真を受け取りに来ました。
shashin o uketori ni kimashita

I've got a problem with my camera
カメラの調子がおかしいです。
kamera no chôshi ga okashî desu

I don't know what it is
何かわかりません。
nani ka wakarimasen

the flash doesn't work
フラッシュが出ません。
furasshu ga demasen

Understanding

一時間現像 *ichi jikan genzô*	photos developed in one hour
標準版 *hyôjunban*	standard format
特急サービス *tokkyû sâbisu*	express service
CDに保存した写真 *shîdî ni hozon shita shashin*	photos on CD

電池が切れたんだと思います。
denchi ga kireta n da to omoimasu
maybe the battery's dead

デジタルカメラの印刷できます。
dejitaru kamera no insatsu dekimasu
we have a machine for printing digital photos

お名前は。
onamae wa?
what's the name, please?

いつ、お受け取りをご希望ですか。
itsu ouketori o gokibô desu ka?
when do you want them for?

一時間で現像できます。
ichi jikan de genzô dekimasu
we can develop them in an hour

BANKS	

It is strongly advised to change money before you go to Japan. There are not many bureaux de change, and those there are (found inside branches of the major banks) are only open during the week from 9am to 3pm. Even though other forms of payment are possible in Japan, there is an overwhelming tendency to pay by cash. Only shops and restaurants in the major cities accept cards, and travellers' cheques are not usually accepted.

Few cash dispensers take international Visa® cards or MasterCard®, even in Tokyo, except those of the **Sumitomo-Mitsui** bank (featuring a green flag divided into three) or **Citibank** (a white star on a blue circle). Even these usually have limited opening hours. However, over 21,000 post offices now have ATMs that accept foreign credit, debit and cash cards. Opening hours of ATMs at large branches are 7am to 11pm on weekdays and 9am to 7pm on weekends and national holidays, but they are more restricted in smaller branches. See the following website for information on cards accepted by post office cash dispensers: http://www.yu-cho.japanpost.jp/e_a0000000/aa200000.htm

The basics

ATM	ATM êtîemu
bank	銀行 ginkô
bank account	銀行口座 ginkô kôza
banknote	紙幣 shihê, お札 osatsu
bureau de change	両替所 ryôgaejo
cashpoint	現金自動支払機 genkin jidô shiharaiki
change	おつり otsuri
cheque	小切手 kogitte
coin	硬貨 kôka
commission	手数料 tesûryô
PIN	暗証番号 anshô bangô
Travellers Cheques®	トラベラーズチェック toraberâzu chekku
withdrawal	引き出し hikidashi

BANKS

to change	両替する ryôgae suru
to transfer	（口座に）振り込む furikomu
to withdraw	引き出す hikidasu, おろす orosu

The different denominations

円 en	yen
一円硬貨 ichi en kôka	1-yen coin
五円硬貨 go en kôka	5-yen coin
十円硬貨 jû en kôka	10-yen coin
五十円硬貨 gojû en kôka	50-yen coin
百円硬貨 hyaku en kôka	100-yen coin
五百円硬貨 gohyaku en kôka	500-yen coin
千円札 sen en satsu	1,000-yen note
二千円札 nisen en satsu	2,000-yen note
五千円札 gosen en satsu	5,000-yen note
一万円札 ichiman en satsu	10,000-yen note

Expressing yourself

where I can get some money changed?
両替はどこでできますか。
ryôgae wa doko de dekimasu ka?

are banks open on Saturdays?
銀行は土曜日も開いていますか。
ginkô wa doyôbi mo aite imasu ka?

I'm looking for a cashpoint
ＡＴＭはどこにありますか。
êtîemu wa doko ni arimasu ka?

I'd like to change £100
100ポンド、両替したいんですが。
hyaku pondo, ryôgae shitai n desu ga

what commission do you charge?
手数料はいくらですか。
tesûryô wa ikura desu ka?

I'd like to transfer some money
お金を振り込みたいんですが。
okane o furikomitai n desu ga

I'd like to report the loss of my credit card
クレジットカード紛失の届けをしたいんですが。
kurejitto kâdo funshitsu no todoke o shitai n desu ga

the cashpoint has swallowed my card
ＡＴＭからカードが戻ってきません。
êtîemu kara kâdo ga modotte kimasen

Understanding

カードを挿入してください。
kâdo o sônyû shite kudasai
please insert your card

暗証番号を入力してください。
anshô bangô o nyûryoku shite kudasai
please enter your PIN number

引き出し金額を入力してください。
hikidashi kingaku o nyûryoku shite kudasai
please select amount for withdrawal

レシートを発行する。
reshîto o hakkô suru
withdrawal with receipt

レシートを発行しない。
reshîto o hakkô shinai
withdrawal without receipt

金額を選んでください。
kingaku o erande kudasai
please select the amount you require

故障中。
koshô chû
out of service

POST OFFICES

Post offices can be recognized by the symbol 〒, and are open Monday to Friday from 9am to 5pm. Letter boxes are red, and those marked 手紙 *tegami* or はがき *hagaki* are for regular mail and domestic deliveries, while those marked その他の郵便 *sono ta no yûbin* are for international and urgent mail.

Stamps are sold at post offices but also in nearby minimarkets and **kombini** (see p. 90). There are different rates for letters and postcards, and for deliveries within Japan and abroad.

The basics

airmail	航空便 *kôkûbin*
commemorative stamp	記念切手 *kinen kitte*
envelope	封筒 *fûtô*
express delivery	速達 *sokutatsu*
letter	手紙 *tegami*
mail	郵便 *yûbin*
parcel	小包 *kozutsumi*
post	郵便 *yûbin*
postbox	ポスト *posuto*
postcard	はがき *hagaki*
postcode	郵便番号 *yûbin bangô*
post office	郵便局 *yûbinkyoku*
registered mail	書留 *kakitome*
sea mail	船便 *funabin*
stamp	切手 *kitte*
to post	投函する *tôkan suru*
to send	送る *okuru*
to write	書く *kaku*

Expressing yourself

is there a post office around here?
この近くに郵便局はありますか。
kono chikaku ni yûbinkyoku wa arimasu ka?

is there a postbox near here?
この近くにポストはありますか。
kono chikaku ni posuto wa arimasu ka?

is the post office open on Saturdays?
郵便局は土曜日も開いていますか。
yûbinkyoku wa doyôbi mo aite imasu ka?

what time does the post office close?
郵便局は何時に閉まりますか。
yûbinkyoku wa nan ji ni shimarimasu ka?

do you sell stamps?
切手はありますか。
kitte wa arimasu ka?

I'd like … stamps for the UK, please
イギリスへの切手を … 枚ください。
igirisu e no kitte o … mai kudasai

how long will it take to arrive?
着くのにどれくらいかかりますか。
tsuku no ni dore kurai kakarimasu ka?

where can I buy envelopes?
封筒はどこで買えますか。
fûtô wa doko de kaemasu ka?

is there any post for me?
私あての郵便物はありますか。
watashi ate no yûbinbutsu wa arimasu ka?

Making sense of addresses

When addresses are written in roman letters, they follow the same pattern as those written in English. When they are written in Japanese, however, the order is reversed as follows: postcode, region, town, area, street, house or apartment and room number, and finally the addressee's name with the suffix **sama**. The postcode is preceded by the symbol 〒.

Understanding

こわれもの *kowaremono*	fragile
取扱い注意 *toriatsukai chûi*	handle with care
受取人 *uketorinin*	recipient
SAL便 *saru bin*	SAL (Economy Air: cheaper than airmail but quicker than surface mail)
送り主 *okurinushi*, 差出人 *sashidashinin*	sender

三日から五日かかります。
mikka kara itsuka kakarimasu
it'll take between three and five days

保険をおかけになりますか。
hoken o okake ni narimasu ka
would you like to insure it?

Delivery services 宅配便 *takuhaibin*

Domestic door-to-door delivery services such as **Kuroneko-Yamato Takkyûbin** and **Sagawa Kyûbin** deliver parcels and packages within Japan very quickly, reliably and often more cheaply than the post office. You can even use them to send your luggage ahead of you, for example, to the airport if you allow a few days before your departure. Hotels and many convenience stores deal with these companies.

INTERNET CAFÉS AND E-MAIL

Exchanging e-mail addresses is common in Japan, and there are plenty of Internet cafés in cities, particularly in the trendy areas. You may need to become a member, but this is a simple procedure. If they can't get to a computer, young people often e-mail each other via their mobile phones, each of which has its own e-mail address. The Japanese use an adapted English keyboard, on which the keys have both roman and Japanese characters (using the *hiragana* writing system) – so, for example, you would find A and あ on the same key. You can select English or Japanese entry on-screen. The icon for this can differ so it's best to ask for help.

The basics

at sign	アットマーク *atto mâku*
e-mail	E メール *îmêru*, 電子メール *denshi mêru*
e-mail address	メールアドレス *mêru adoresu*
Internet café	インターネットカフェ *intânetto kafe*
keyboard	キーボード *kîbôdo*
key	キー *kî*
save	保存 *hozon*
to copy	コピー *copî*
to cut	切り取り *kiritori*
to delete	削除 *sakujo*
to download	ダウンロード *daunrôdo*
to e-mail somebody	メールを送る *mêru o okuru*
to paste	貼り付け *haritsuke*
to print	印刷 *insatsu*
to receive	受信 *jushin*
to save	保存する *hozon suru*
to send an e-mail	送信 *sôshin*

109

Expressing yourself

is there an Internet café near here?
この近くにインターネットカフェはありますか。
kono chikaku ni intânetto kafe wa arimasu ka?

do you have an e-mail address?
メールアドレスはありますか。
mêru adoresu wa arimasu ka?

how do I get online?
どうしたらネットワークに接続できますか。
dô shitara nettowâku ni setsuzoku dekimasu ka?

I'd just like to check my e-mails
自分のメールをチェックしたいんですが。
jibun no mêru o chekku shitai n desu ga

would you mind helping me, I'm not sure what to do
どうしたらいいのか分かりません。ちょっと手伝ってもらえません
か。
dô shitara î no ka wakarimasen. chotto tetsudatte moraemasen ka?

I can't find the at sign on this keyboard
アットマークがどこにあるかわかりません。
atto mâku ga doko ni aru ka wakarimasen

it's not working
動きません。
ugokimasen

there's something wrong with the computer, it's frozen
コンピュータがおかしいです。固まってしまいました。
kompyûta ga okashî desu. katamatte shimaimashita

how much will it be for half an hour?
30分でいくらですか。
sanjippun de ikura desu ka?

when do I pay?
いつ払ったらいいですか。
itsu harattara î desu ka?

how do I type in English?
どうしたら英語で打てますか。
dô shitara êgo de utemasu ka?

Understanding

添付 *tempu*		attach
受信トレイ *jushin torê*		inbox
送信トレイ *sôshin torê*		outbox

会員カードはお持ちですか。
kai-in kâdo wa omochi desu ka?
do you have a membership card?

会員になられますか。
kai-in ni nararemasu ka?
would you like to become a member?

身分証明書はお持ちですか。
mibunshômêsho wa omochi desu ka?
do you have proof of identity?

禁煙ブースをご利用になられますか。
kin'en bûsu o goriyô ni nararemasu ka?
would you like a non-smoking booth?

20分ぐらいお待ちいただきます。
nijippun gurai omachi itadakimasu
you'll have to wait for 20 minutes or so

分からないことがあったら、お尋ねください。
wakaranai koto ga attara, otazune kudasai
just ask if you're not sure what to do

ログオンするのには、このパスワードを入力してください。
roguon suru no ni wa, kono pasuwâdo o nyûryoku shite kudasai
just enter this password to log on

So many people have mobile phones in Japan that using phone booths is rare. Nevertheless, phone booths have been modernized and most now take **IC** cards instead of the old **NTT** ones. Phonecards are sold at kiosks and **kombini** (see p. 90), or from vending machines inside the booth itself. Payphones in cafés usually only take coins. To call the UK from Japan, dial 001 44 followed by the phone number, including the area code but omitting the first zero. The international dialling code for Ireland is 001 353, and for the US and Canada it is 0011. To call Japan from abroad, dial 00 81 followed by the area code and number, omitting the first zero.

Most UK mobile phones don't work in Japan, although some new models do; it's best to check with your phone company. It is possible to hire Japanese mobile phones from companies in the UK, or at the major international airports after arriving in Japan.

Phone numbers are read out one digit at a time. When writing a phone number, the different elements are separated by hyphens: for example, in the number 03-1234-5678, the 03 stands for Tokyo, the 1234 is the area, and 5678 the person's number. "0" is pronounced as *zero* or *rê*.

The basics

answering machine	留守番電話 *rusuban denwa*
call	電話 *denwa*
directory enquiries	番号案内 *bangô annai*
hello	もしもし *moshi moshi*
international call	国際電話 *kokusai denwa*
local call	市内電話 *shinai denwa*
message	伝言 *dengon*, メッセージ *messêji*
mobile	携帯（電話）*kêtai (denwa)*
national call	市外電話 *shigai denwa*
phone	電話 *denwa*
phone book	電話帳 *denwa chô*
phone box	電話ボックス *denwa bokkusu*

phone call	電話 *denwa*
phonecard	テレホンカード *terehon kâdo*
phone number	電話番号 *denwa bangô*
public phone	公衆電話 *kôshû denwa*
ringtone	着メロ *chaku mero*
telephone	電話 *denwa*
Yellow Pages ®	タウンページ *taun pêji*
to call somebody	電話する *denwa suru*, 電話をかける *denwa o kakeru*

Expressing yourself

where can I buy a phonecard?
テレホンカードはどこで買えますか。
terehon kâdo wa doko de kaemasu ka?

I'd like to make a reverse-charge call
コレクトコールをお願いします。
korekuto kôru o onegai shimasu

is there a phone box near here, please?
この近くに電話ボックスはありますか。
kono chikaku ni denwa bokkusu wa arimasu ka?

can I plug my phone in here to recharge it?
携帯の充電をここでしてもいいですか。
kêtai no jûden o koko de shite mo î desu ka?

do you have a mobile number?
携帯の番号はありますか。
kêtai no bangô wa arimasu ka?

where can I contact you?
どこへ連絡したらいいですか。
doko e renraku shitara î desu ka?

did you get my message?
私の伝言は聞いてもらえましたか。
watashi no dengon wa kîte moraemashita ka?

Understanding

おかけになった電話番号は、ただいま使われておりません。
okake ni natta denwa bangô wa tadaima tsukawarete orimasen
the number you have dialled has not been recognized

シャープボタンを押してください。
shâpu botan o oshite kudasai
please press the hash key

MAKING A CALL

Expressing yourself

hello, this is David Brown (speaking)
もしもし、デイヴィッド・ブラウンですが。
moshi moshi, dêviddo buraun desu ga

hello, could I speak to ..., please?
もしもし、... さんはいらっしゃいますか。
moshi moshi, ... san wa irasshaimasu ka?

hello, is that Mr/Ms Tanaka?
もしもし、田中さんですか。
moshimoshi, tanaka-san desu ka?

do you speak English?
英語は話せますか。
êgo wa hanasemasu ka?

could you speak more slowly, please?
もう少しゆっくり話してくれますか。
mô sukoshi yukkuri hanashite kuremasu ka?

I can't hear you, could you speak up, please?
すみませんが、よく聞こえません。もう少し大きな声で話してくれ
ませんか。
*sumimasen ga, yoku kikoemasen. mô sukoshi ôkina koe de hanashite
kuremasen ka?*

TELEPHONE

could you tell him/her I called?
私から電話があったと伝えてもらえますか。
watashi kara denwa ga atta to tsutaete moraemasu ka?

could you ask him/her to call me back?
電話をしてくれるように伝えてもらえますか。
denwa o shite kureru yô ni tsutaete moraemasu ka?

I'll call back later
また後でかけ直します。
mata ato de kakenaoshimasu

my name is … and my number is …
… と申しますが、電話番号は … です。
… to môshimasu ga, denwa bangô wa … desu

do you know when he/she might be available?
いつでしたら、連絡がつきますか。
itsu deshitara, renraku ga tsukimasu ka?

thank you, goodbye
では、失礼します。
dewa, shitsurê shimasu

Understanding

どちら様でしょうか。
dochira sama deshô ka?
who's calling?

電話番号をお間違えではありませんか。
denwa bangô o omachigae de wa arimasen ka?
you've got the wrong number

ただいま、外出しております。　伝言をお伝えしましょうか。
tadaima gaishutsu shite orimasu　*dengon o otsutae shimashô ka?*
he's/she's not here at the moment　do you want to leave a message?

お電話があったことをお伝えいたします。
odenwa ga atta koto o otsutae shimasu
I'll tell him/her you called

電話をかけるように伝えます。
denwa o kakeru yô ni tsutaemasu
I'll ask him/her to call you back

少々、お待ちください。
shôshô omachi kudasai
hold on

ただいま替わります。
tadaima kawarimasu
I'll just hand you over to him/her

PROBLEMS

Expressing yourself

I don't know the code
局番がわかりません。
kyoku ban ga wakarimasen

it's engaged
話し中です。
hanashi chû desu

there's no reply
誰も出ません。
dare mo demasen

I couldn't get through
つながりませんでした。
tsunagarimasen deshita

my phonecard has almost run out
テレホンカードが終わりそうです。
terehon kâdo ga owarisô desu

we're about to get cut off
もうすぐ、切れます。
môsugu kiremasu

the reception's really bad
受信状態がとても悪いです。
jushin jôtai ga totemo warui desu

I can't hear you very well
よく聞こえないんですが。
yoku kikoenai n desu ga

I can't get a signal
圏外のようです。
kengai no yô desu

Understanding

何を言っているか聞こえません。
nani o itte iru ka kikoemasen
I can hardly hear you

雑音がひどいです。
zatsuon ga hidoi desu
it's a bad line

HEALTH

Chemist's are open every day from 10am to 7pm. There are no emergency pharmacies but some hospitals do provide 24-hour cover. There is no GP system in Japan, and it is common to go straight to the hospital to see a specialist instead of seeing a doctor, even for minor problems. The emergency number is **119**.

Signs saying 薬局 *yakkyoku* (chemist's) and 薬 *kusuri* (medicines) are used for both small chemist's and the health counters in some hypermarkets or the specialist chain **Matsumoto Kiyoshi**. Medicines available without prescription include those for headaches (頭痛薬 *zutsûyaku*), fever (解熱剤 *genetsuzai*), sore throats (のどの痛み止め *nodo no itamidome*), period pain (生理痛の薬 *sêritsû no kusuri*), diarrhoea (下痢止め *geridome*) and constipation (下剤 *gezai*).

Make sure you take out health insurance for your trip, and keep receipts for treatment so you can be reimbursed.

The basics

allergy	アレルギー *arerugî*
ambulance	救急車 *kyûkyûsha*
appendicitis	盲腸炎 *môchôen*
aspirin	アスピリン *asupirin*
asthma	喘息 *zensoku*
blood	血 *chi*, 血液 *ketsueki*
broken	折れた *oreta*, 骨折した *kossetsu shita*
casualty (department)	救急病院 *kyûkyû byôin*
chemist's	薬局 *yakkyoku*, 薬屋 *kusuriya*
cold	風邪 *kaze*
condom	コンドーム *kondômu*
dentist	歯医者 *haisha*, 歯科医 *shikai*
diarrhoea	下痢 *geri*
doctor	医者 *isha*
flu	インフルエンザ *infuruenza*
food poisoning	食中毒 *shokuchûdoku*

gynaecologist	婦人科 fujinka
hay fever	花粉症 kafunshô
headache	頭痛 zutsû
hospital	病院 byôin
infection	感染 kansen
insect bite	虫刺され mushisasare
medicine	薬 kusuri
painkiller	鎮痛剤 chintsûzai, 痛み止め itamidome
periods	生理 sêri
plaster	絆創膏 bansôkô
rash	発疹 hasshin
spot	吹き出物 fukidemono
sunburn	ひどい日焼け hidoi hiyake
surgical spirit	消毒用アルコール shôdoku yô arukôru
tablet	錠剤 jôzai
temperature	熱 netsu
vaccination	予防接種 yobôsesshu
vaccine	ワクチン wakuchin
x-ray	レントゲン rentogen
to disinfect	消毒する shôdoku suru
to faint	失神する shisshin suru
to vomit	吐く haku

Expressing yourself

does anyone have an aspirin/a tampon/a plaster, by any chance?
誰かアスピリン・タンポン・絆創膏を持っていませんか。
dare ka asupirin/tampon/bansôkô o motte imasen ka?

I need to see a doctor
お医者さんに診てもらわなければなりません。
oisha-san ni mite morawanakereba narimasen

where can I find a doctor?
お医者さんはどこにいますか。
oisha-san wa doko ni imasu ka?

I'd like to make an appointment for today
今日の診察の予約をしたいんですが。
kyô no shinsatsu no yoyaku o shitai n desu ga

as soon as possible
できるだけ早く。
dekiru dake hayaku

no, it doesn't matter
いいえ、それは大丈夫です。
îe, sore wa daijôbu desu

can you send an ambulance to …
… へ救急車をお願いします。
… e kyûkyûsha o onegai shimasu

I've broken my glasses
メガネを壊してしまいました。
megane o kowashite shimaimashita

I've lost a contact lens
コンタクトレンズを失くしてしまいました。
kontakuto renzu o nakushite shimaimashita

Understanding

救急病院 *kyûkyû byôin*	casualty department
診療所・医院 *shinsatsujo/i-in*	doctor's surgery
処方箋 *shohôsen*	prescription

木曜日まで予約はいっぱいです。
mokuyôbi made yoyaku wa ippai desu
there are no available appointments until Thursday

金曜日の午後２時はいかがですか。
kin'yôbi no gogo ni ji wa ikaga desu ka?
is Friday at 2pm OK?

AT THE DOCTOR'S OR THE HOSPITAL

Expressing yourself

I have an appointment with Dr …
… 先生に予約してあります。
… sensê ni yoyaku shite arimasu

I don't feel very well
気分があまりよくありません。
kibun ga amari yoku arimasen

I feel very weak
力が出ません。
chikara ga demasen

I don't know what it is
何かわかりません。
nani ka wakarimasen

I've got a headache
頭が痛いです。
atama ga itai desu

I've got a sore throat
のどが痛いです。
nodo ga itai desu

my back hurts
背中・腰が痛いです。
senaka (upper back)/koshi (lower back) ga itai desu

it hurts
痛いです。
itai desu

I feel sick
吐き気がします。
hakike ga shimasu

it's got worse
だんだん悪くなってきました。
dandan waruku natte kimashita

it started last night
夕べから始まりました。
yûbe kara hajimarimashita

it's never happened to me before
こんなことは初めてです。
konna koto wa hajimete desu

I've got a temperature
熱があります。
netsu ga arimasu

I have a heart condition
心臓の持病があります。
shinzô no jibyô ga arimasu

I've been bitten/stung by ...
... にかまれました・刺されました。
... ni kamaremashita/sasaremashita

I've got toothache/stomachache
歯が・おなかが痛いです。
ha ga/onaka ga itai desu

it hurts here
ここが痛いです。
koko ga itai desu

I'm diabetic
糖尿病です。
tônyôbyô desu

it's been three days
もう3日間、こうです。
mô mikka kan kô desu

I have asthma
喘息があります。
zensoku ga arimasu

it itches
かゆいです。
kayui desu

I've been on antibiotics for a week and I'm not getting any better
抗生物質を一週間飲んでいますが、よくなりません。
kôsêbusshitsu o isshûkan nonde imasu ga, yoku narimasen

I'm on the pill/the minipill
ピル・ミニピルを飲んでいます。
piru/minipiru o nonde imasu

I'm ... months pregnant
妊娠 ... ヶ月です。
ninshin ... ka getsu desu

I'm allergic to penicillin
ペニシリンのアレルギーがあります。
penishirin no arerugî ga arimasu

I've twisted my ankle
足首をひねりました。
ashikubi o hinerimashita

I fell and hurt my back
落ちて腰を痛めました。
ochite koshi o itamemashita

I've had a blackout
一瞬、気を失いました。
isshun ki o ushinaimashita

I've lost a filling
歯の詰め物がとれました。
ha no tsumemono ga toremashita

I don't want the tooth extracted
歯を抜かないでください。
ha o nukanaide kudasai

is it serious?
かなり重いですか。
kanari omoi desu ka?

is it contagious?
うつりますか。
utsurimasu ka?

how is he/she?
様子はどうですか。
yôsu wa dô desu ka?

how much do I owe you?
おいくらですか。
oikura desu ka?

can I have a receipt so I can get the money refunded?
払い戻してもらうので、領収書をもらえませんか。
haraimodoshite morau node, ryôshûsho o moraemasen ka?

Understanding

待合室でお待ちください。
machiaishitsu de omachi kudasai
if you'd like to take a seat in the waiting room

どこが痛みますか。
doko ga itamimasu ka?
where does it hurt?

深く息をしてください。
fukaku iki o shite kudasai
take a deep breath

横になってください。
yoko ni natte kudasai
lie down, please

ここを押すと痛みますか。
koko o osu to itamimasu ka?
does it hurt when I press here?

… にアレルギーがありますか。
… ni arerugî ga arimasu ka?
are you allergic to …?

他に薬を飲んでいますか。
hoka ni kusuri o nonde imasu ka?
are you taking any other medication?

… の予防接種はしましたか。
… no yobôsesshu wa shimashita ka?
have you been vaccinated against …?

処方箋を出しておきます。
shohôsen o dashite okimasu
I'm going to write you a prescription

すぐ治るはずです。
sugu naoru hazu desu
it should heal quickly

手術が必要です。
shujutsu ga hitsuyô desu
you're going to need an operation

一週間後にもう一度来てください。
isshû kan go ni mô ichi do kite kudasai
come back and see me in a week

数日のうちによくなるはずです。
sû nichi no uchi ni yoku naru hazu desu
it should clear up in a few days

AT THE CHEMIST'S

Expressing yourself

I'd like a box of plasters, please
絆創膏を一箱ください。
bansôkô o hito hako kudasai

could I have something for a bad cold?
ひどい風邪を引きました。薬をください。
hidoi kaze o hikimashita. kusuri o kudasai

I need something for a cough
セキの薬をください。
seki no kusuri o kudasai

I'm allergic to aspirin
アスピリンのアレルギーがあります。
asupirin no arerugî ga arimasu

I'd like a bottle of solution for soft contact lenses
ソフトコンタクトレンズの保存液をください。
sofuto kontakuto renzu no hozon eki o kudasai

Understanding

塗る *nuru*	apply
処方箋が必要 *shohôsen ga hitsuyô*	available on prescription only
食前・食後・食間 *shoku zen/shoku go/shokkan*	before/after/between meals
カプセル *kapuseru*	capsule
禁忌 *kinki*	contra-indications
クリーム *kurîmu*	cream
軟膏 *nankô*	ointment
副作用の可能性 *fukusayô no kanôsê*	possible side effects
散薬 *san'yaku*	powder
座薬 *zayaku*	suppositories
シロップ剤 *shiroppu zai*	syrup
錠剤 *jôzai*	tablet

一日３回、食前にお飲みください。
ichi nichi san kai, shoku zen ni onomi kudasai
take three times a day before meals

HEALTH

PROBLEMS AND EMERGENCIES

In an emergency dial **110** for police and **119** for the fire brigade or an ambulance. Note that if you dial 119 you will need to specify which service you require: *shôbôsha o onegai shimasui* for the fire brigade or *kyûkyûsha o onegai shimasu* for an ambulance.

Japan has a system of local police boxes/offices (**kôban**) open 24 hours a day, where the neighbourhood police officers (**omawari-san**) are based. If you need to ask directions or have lost something, or there is some kind of emergency, this is a good place to go.

Note that when it comes to filling in paperwork and so on, the Japanese use seals instead of signatures, and you may be asked for a thumbprint if you don't have a seal.

The basics

accident	事故 *jiko*
ambulance	救急車 *kyûkyûsha*
broken	折れた *oreta*, 骨折した *kossetsu shita*
coastguard	沿岸警備隊 *engan kêbitai*
disabled	障害者 *shôgaisha*
doctor	医者 *isha*
emergency	緊急 *kinkyû*
fire brigade	消防隊 *shôbôtai*
fire	火事 *kaji*
hospital	病院 *byôin*
ill	病気 *byôki*
injury	怪我 *kega*
late	遅い *osoi*
police	警察 *kêsatsu*
police box	交番 *kôban*

Expressing yourself

can you help me?
手伝ってくれませんか。
tetsudatte kuremasen ka?

earthquake!
地震だ
jishin da!

help!
助けて
tasukete!

fire!
火事だ
kaji da!

be careful!
気をつけろ
ki o tsukero!

it's an emergency!
緊急です
kinkyû desu!

could I borrow your phone, please?
電話を貸してもらえませんか。
denwa o kashite moraemasen ka?

there's been an accident
事故がありました。
jiko ga arimashita

does anyone here speak English?
英語が話せる人はいませんか。
êgo ga hanaseru hito wa imasen ka?

I need to contact the British consulate/embassy
英国領事館・大使館に連絡しなければなりません。
êkoku ryôjikan/taishikan ni renraku shinakereba narimasen

where's the nearest police station?
一番近い警察署はどこですか。
ichiban chikai kêsatsusho wa doko desu ka?

what do I have to do?
どうしたらいいですか。
dô shitara î desu ka?

my passport/credit card has been stolen
パスポート・クレジットカードを盗まれました。
pasupôto/kurejitto kâdo o nusumaremashita

my bag's been snatched
かばんをひったくられました。
kaban o hittakuraremashita

I've lost …
… を失くしました。
… o nakushimashita

I'm lost
道に迷いました。
michi ni mayoimashita

I've been attacked
襲われました。
osowaremashita

my son/daughter is missing
息子・娘がいなくなりました。
musuko/musume ga inaku narimashita

my car's been towed away
車がレッカー車に持っていかれました。
kuruma ga rekkâsha ni motte ikaremashita

I've broken down
車が故障しました。
kuruma ga koshô shimashita

my car's been broken into
車上荒らしにあいました。
shajôarashi ni aimashita

there's a man following me
私の後をつけてくる男の人がいます。
watashi no ato o tsukete kuru otoko no hito ga imasu

is there disabled access?
障害者が使えるようになっていますか。
shôgaisha ga tsukaeru yô ni natte imasu ka?

can you keep an eye on my things for a minute?
ちょっと荷物を見ていてくれますか。
chotto nimotsu o mite ite kuremasu ka?

he's drowning, get help!
人が溺れています。助けて
hito ga oborete imasu. tasukete!

Understanding

猛犬注意 *môken chûi*	beware of the dog
故障修理 *koshô shûri*	breakdown service
非常口 *hijôguchi*	emergency exit
落し物・遺失物 *otoshimono/ ishitsubutsu*	lost property
山岳救助隊 *sangaku kyûjotai*	mountain rescue
故障中 *koshô chû*	out of order

POLICE

Expressing yourself

I want to report something stolen
盗難の届け出をしたいんですが。
tônan no todokede o shitai n desu ga

I need a document from the police for my insurance company
保険請求のため、警察の証明書が要ります。
hoken sêkyû no tame, kêsatsu no shômêsho ga irimasu

Understanding

Filling in forms

姓・名字 sê/myôji	surname
名・名前 mê/namae	given name
住所 jûsho	address
郵便番号 yûbin bangô	postcode
国 kuni	country
国籍 kokuseki	nationality
生年月日 sênengappi	date of birth
出生地 shussêchi	place of birth
年齢 nenrê	age
性別 sêbetsu	sex
滞在期間 taizai kikan	duration of stay
入国・出国日 nyûkoku/shukkoku bi	arrival/departure date
職業 shokugyô	occupation
旅券番号 ryoken bangô	passport number

この品物には関税がかかります。
kono shinamono ni wa kanzê ga kakarimasu
there's customs duty to pay on this item

かばんを開けてください。
kaban o akete kudasai
would you open this bag, please?

何がなくなっていますか。
nani ga naku natte imasu ka?
what's missing?

いつ起きましたか。
itsu okimashita ka?
when did this happen?

どこに泊まっていますか。
doko ni tomatte imasu ka?
where are you staying?

どんな人・ものですか。
donna hito (him/her)/mono (it) desu ka?
can you describe him/her/it?

この用紙に記入してください。
kono yôshi ni kinyû shite kudasai
would you fill in this form, please?

ここに署名・サインしてください。
koko ni shomê/sain shite kudasai
would you sign here, please?

ここに拇印を押してください。
koko ni boin o oshite kudasai
would you give your thumbprint here, please?

Some informal expressions

おまわり（さん）*omawari (san)* cop
ブタ箱 *butabako* slammer, nick
パクられる *pakurareru* to get nicked
盗まれる *nusumareru* to get something nicked

TIME AND DATE

The basics

after	… の後で … no ato de
already	もう mô
always	いつも itsumo
at lunchtime	昼食の時間 chûshoku no jikan
at the beginning/ end of	… の始めに・終わりに … no hajime ni/owari ni
at the moment	今のところ ima no tokoro
before	… の前に … no mae ni
between ... and ...	… と … の間 … to … no aida
day	日 nichi/hi
daytime	昼間 hiruma
during	… の間 … no aida
early	早い hayai
early evening	夕方 yûgata
for a long time	長い間 nagai aida
from ... to ...	… から … まで … kara … made
from time to time	ときどき tokidoki
in a little while	まもなく mamonaku
in the evening	(early) 夕方 yûgata; (late) 夜 yoru
in the middle of	… の最中 … no saichû
last	前の mae no
late	(in time) 遅い osoi; (behind schedule) 遅れて okurete
late evening	夜 yoru, 晩 ban
midday	正午 shôgo
midnight	真夜中 mayonaka
morning	朝 asa, 午前中 gozen chû
month	月 tsuki/getsu
never	決して … ない kesshite … nai
next	次の tsugi no
not yet	まだ … ない mada … nai
now	今 ima
occasionally	時折 tokiori
often	よく yoku

rarely	めったに … ない *metta ni … nai*
recently	最近 *saikin*
since	… から … *kara*
sometimes	ときどき *tokidoki*
soon	すぐ *sugu*
still	まだ *mada*
straightaway	ただちに *tadachi ni*, すぐに *sugu ni*
until	… まで *made*
week	週 *shû*
weekend	週末 *shûmatsu*
year	年 *toshi/nen*

Expressing yourself

see you soon!
じゃ、また。
ja, mata

see you later!
また、後で。
mata ato de

see you on Monday!
月曜日に会いましょう。
getsuyôbi ni aimashô

have a good weekend!
よい週末を。
yoi shûmatsu o

sorry I'm late
遅れてすみません。
okurete sumimasen

I've never been there
まだ行ったことがありません。
mada itta koto ga arimasen

I haven't had time to …
… する時間がありませんでした。
… suru jikan ga arimasen deshita

I've got plenty of time
時間はたっぷりあります。
jikan wa tappuri arimasu

I'm in a rush
急いでいます。
isoide imasu

hurry up!
急いで。
isoide!

just a minute, please
ちょっと待ってください。
chotto matte kudasai

I had a late night
昨日は夜遅かったんです。
kinô wa yoru osokatta n desu

I got up very early
とても早く起きました。
totemo hayaku okimashita

I waited ages
ずいぶん待ちました。
zuibun machimashita

we only have four days left
あと4日しかありません。
ato yokka shika arimasen

I have to get up very early tomorrow to catch my plane
飛行機に乗るので、明日はすごく早く起きなければなりません。
hikôki ni noru node ashita wa sugoku hayaku okinakereba narimasen

THE DATE

The date can be written in two different ways, depending on whether it relates to the Western or Japanese calendar; the latter is based on imperial reigns. It is always written year (年 *nen*), month (月 *gatsu*), day (日 *nichi*). For example, 2006 年 3 月 15 日 (15 March 2006) would be equivalent to 平成18年 (18th year of the Heisei era).

The symbol 日 (day) is pronounced differently depending on whether it refers to a day of the week (Monday, Tuesday etc), a day of the month (1st May, 2nd May etc) or a period of time relating to a particular day (today, yesterday, the day before yesterday etc). The same applies to the symbol 月 (month). The system for counting days and months combines Japanese numbers (1 to 10, with a few exceptions) and Chinese numbers (see p. 139).

The basics

... ago	… 前 … *mae*
in two days' time	2日後 *futsuka go*
last night	昨夜 *sakuya,* ゆうべ *yûbe*
last week/month/year	先週・先月・去年 *sen shû/sen getsu/kyo nen*
next week/month/year	来週・来月・来年 *rai shû/rai getsu/rai nen*
the day before yesterday	おととい *ototoi*
this evening	今晩 *komban*
this morning	今朝 *kesa*

this week/month/year	今週・今月・今年 *kon shû/kon getsu/kotoshi*
today	今日 *kyô*
tomorrow	明日 *ashita*
tomorrow morning/afternoon/ evening	明日の朝・午後・夕方 *ashita no asa/gogo/yûgata*
yesterday	昨日 *kinô*
yesterday morning/afternoon/ evening	昨日の朝・午後・夕方 *kinô no asa/gogo/yûgata*

Days of the week

Monday	月曜日	*getsuyôbi*
Tuesday	火曜日	*kayôbi*
Wednesday	水曜日	*suiyôbi*
Thursday	木曜日	*mokuyôbi*
Friday	金曜日	*kin'yôbi*
Saturday	土曜日	*doyôbi*
Sunday	日曜日	*nichiyôbi*

Dates

Dates from 11th to 19th: number + 日 *nichi*
Number of days from 11 to 19 and 21 to 31: number + 日間 *nichi kan*

1st	一日 *tsuitachi*		**1 day**	一日中 *ichi nichi*
2nd	二日 *futsuka*		**2 days**	二日間 *futsuka kan*
3rd	三日 *mikka*		**3 days**	三日間 *mikka kan*
4th	四日 *yokka*		**4 days**	四日間 *yokka kan*
5th	五日 *itsuka*		**5 days**	五日間 *itsuka kan*
6th	六日 *muika*		**6 days**	六日間 *muika kan*
7th	七日 *nanoka*		**7 days**	七日間 *nanoka kan*
8th	八日 *yôka*		**8 days**	八日間 *yôka kan*
9th	九日 *kokonoka*		**9 days**	九日間 *kokonoka kan*
10th	十日 *tôka*		**10 days**	十日間 *tôka kan*
11th	十一日 *jûichi nichi*		**11 days**	十一日間 *jûichi nichi kan*
14th	十四日 *jûyokka*			
20th	二十日 *hatsuka*			
24th	二十四日 *nijûyokka*			

Months

January	一月 *ichigatsu*
February	二月 *nigatsu*
March	三月 *sangatsu*
April	四月 *shigatsu*
May	五月 *gogatsu*
June	六月 *rokugatsu*
July	七月 *shichigatsu*
August	八月 *hachigatsu*
September	九月 *kugatsu*
October	十月 *jûgatsu*
November	十一月 *jûichigatsu*
December	十二月 *jûnigatsu*

Number of months

1 month	一ヶ月 *ikkagetsu*
2 months	二ヶ月 *nikagetsu*
6 months	六ヶ月 *rokkagetsu*
10 months	十ヶ月 *juikkagetsu*

Expressing yourself

I was born in 1975
1975年に生まれました。
sen kyûhyaku nanajûgo nen ni umaremashita

I came here a few years ago
数年前にここに来ました。
sû nen mae ni koko ni kimashita

I spent a month in Japan last summer
去年の夏、一ヶ月日本にいました。
kyo nen no natsu, ikkagetsu nihon ni imashita

I was here last year at the same time
去年の今頃もここにいました。
kyonen no ima goro mo koko ni imashita

what's the date today?
今日は何日ですか。
kyô wa nan nichi desu ka?

what day is it today?
今日は何曜日ですか。
kyô wa nan yôbi desu ka?

it's the 1st of May
5月1日です。
gogatsu tsuitachi desu

I'm staying until Sunday
日曜日までいます。
nichiyôbi made imasu

we're leaving tomorrow
明日、出発します。
ashita shuppatsu shimasu

I already have plans for Tuesday
火曜日はもう予定があります。
kayôbi wa mô yotê ga arimasu

Understanding

一度 *ichi do,* 一回 *ikkai/*二度 *ni do,* 二回 *ni kai*	once/twice
一時間に三回 *ichi jikan ni san kai/* 一日に三回 *ichi nichi ni san kai*	three times an hour/a day
毎日 *mai nichi*	every day
毎週月曜日 *mai shû getsuyôbi*	every Monday

19世紀の中頃に建てられました。
jûkyû sêki no naka goro ni tateraremashita
it was built in the mid-nineteenth century

ここは夏、とても混みます。
koko wa natsu, totemo komimasu
it gets very busy here in the summer

いつ出発されますか。
itsu shuppatsu saremasu ka?
when are you leaving?

どのくらい滞在されますか。
dono kurai taizai saremasu ka?
how long are you staying?

TIME

The word **ni** is only used when referring to a specific time in hours and minutes: 時に ... *ji ni* ... at ... o'clock. The ending **kan** indicates duration: 時間 ... *jikan* for ... hours. The word **fun** (minute) changes its pronunciation to *pun* following certain numbers.

The words **goro** and **kurai** (or **gurai**) are used with approximate times. *Goro* is used when talking about a point in time: 3時頃 *san ji goro* around 3 o'clock. **Kurai/gurai** refers to duration: 3時間位 *san jikan gurai* for about three hours.

The basics

early	早い *hayai*
half an hour	30分 *sanjippun*
in the afternoon	午後に *gogo ni*
in the morning	朝 *asa*, 午前中に *gozen chû ni*
late	遅い *osoi*, 遅れて *okurete*
midday	正午 *shôgo*
midnight	真夜中 *mayonaka*
on time	時間通りに *jikan dôri ni*
quarter of an hour	15分 *jûgo fun*
three quarters of an hour	45分 *yonjûgo fun*

Expressing yourself

what time is it?
何時ですか。
nan ji desu ka?

excuse me, have you got the time, please?
すみません、時間が分かりますか。
sumimasen, jikan ga wakarimasu ka?

it's exactly three o'clock
ちょうど3時です。
chôdo san ji desu

it's nearly one o'clock
1時近いです。
ichi ji chikai desu

it's ten past one
1時10分です。
ichi ji jippun desu

it's a quarter past one
1時15分です。
ichi ji jûgo fun desu

it's a quarter to one
12時45分です。
jûni ji yonjûgo fun desu

it's twenty past twelve
12時20分です。
jûni ji nijippun desu

it's twenty to twelve
11時40分です。
jûichi ji yonjippun desu

it's half past one
1時半です。
ichi ji han desu

I went to bed about two o' clock
2時ごろ寝ました。
ni ji goro nemashita

I set my alarm for nine
9時に目覚ましをかけておきました。
ku ji ni mezamashi o kakete okimashita

I waited twenty minutes
20分、待ちました。
nijippun machimashita

the train was fifteen minutes late
列車が15分遅れました。
ressha ga jûgo fun okuremashita

I got home an hour ago
一時間前に家に着きました。
ichi jikan mae ni ie ni tsukimashita

shall we meet in half an hour?
30分後に会いましょうか。
sanjippun go ni aimashô ka?

I'll be back in a quarter of an hour
15分後に戻って来ます。
jûgo fun go ni modotte kimasu

there's an eight-hour time difference between the UK and Japan
イギリスと日本の間には8時間、時差があります。
igirisu to nihon no aida ni wa hachi jikan jisa ga arimasu

Understanding

10時から30分毎に出発
jû ji kara sanjippun goto ni shuppatsu
departs every half-hour after ten o'clock

午前10時から午後4時まで営業
gozen jû ji kara gogo yo ji made êgyô
open from 10am to 4pm

毎晩7時からです。
mai ban shichi ji kara desu
it's on every evening at seven

1時間半ぐらいかかります。
ichi jikan han gurai kakarimasu
it lasts around an hour and a half

朝、10時に開きます。
asa jû ji ni akimasu
it opens at ten in the morning

Some informal expressions
2時ぴったりに *ni ji pittari ni* at two o'clock on the dot
8時過ぎたばかりで *hachi ji sugita bakari* it's just gone eight o'clock

The Japanese number system is quite complex – even native speakers get confused sometimes! It combines Japanese and Chinese-derived pronunciations. The Chinese-based ones are used to count numbers and do sums. Various "counters" are added onto these to count objects; the counter depends on the type of objects being counted (see list below). For example, *ko* is used when talking about medium-sized objects (three apples *ringo san ko*); *hon* for long thin objects (two pencils *enpitsu ni hon*), and *mai* for flat objects (three stamps *kitte san mai*). There are also native Japanese numbers for 1 to 10, which can be used to count any type of object; after 10, you need to use the Chinese-based numbers with the appropriate counter. Don't panic though – people will still follow what you're talking about even if you get one of these counters wrong. It's useful to know that *ko* is by far the most commonly used one.

When the item being counted is the direct object of a sentence, the following structure is used: object + *o* + number and counter + verb. For example: *hamu o go mai kudasai* I would like five slices of ham; *kohi o ni hai kudasai* two coffees, please.

While Japanese uses tens, hundreds and thousands as in English, it also uses a larger unit, *man*, for "ten thousand". This means that 30,000 is "three ten thousands" *sam man*; 35,000 is "three ten thousands five thousand" *sam man go sen*; and 1,000,000 is "one hundred ten thousands" *hyaku man*. You need to remember this when shopping!

Japanese numbers

1	ひとつ	*hitotsu*
2	ふたつ	*futatsu*
3	みっつ	*mittsu*
4	よっつ	*yottsu*
5	いつつ	*itsutsu*
6	むっつ	*muttsu*
7	ななつ	*nanatsu*
8	やっつ	*yattsu*

| 9 | ここのつ *kokonotsu* |
| 10 | とお *tô* |

Chinese-based numbers

0	ゼロ *zero*, 零 *rê*
1	一 *ichi*
2	二 *ni*
3	三 *san* (written here and pronounced as *sam* before *m*, *p* and *b*)
4	四 *shi/yon* (written here and pronounced as *yom* before *m*, *f* and *b*)
5	五 *go*
6	六 *roku*
7	七 *shichi/nana*
8	八 *hachi*
9	九 *kyû/ku*
10	十 *jû*
11	十一 *jûichi*
12	十二 *jûni*
13	十三 *jûsan*
14	十四 *jûyon/jûshi*
15	十五 *jûgo*
16	十六 *jûroku*
17	十七 *jûshichi/jûnana*
18	十八 *jûhachi*
19	十九 *jûkyû/jûku*
20	二十 *nijû*
21	二十一 *nijûichi*
22	二十二 *nijûni*
30	三十 *sanjû*
35	三十五 *sanjûgo*
40	四十 *yonjû*
50	五十 *gojû*
60	六十 *rokujû*
70	七十 *nanajû*
80	八十 *hachijû*
90	九十 *kyûjû*
100	百 *hyaku*

101	百一 *hyakuichi*
200	二百 *nihyaku*
300	三百 *sambyaku*
500	五百 *gohyaku*
600	六百 *roppyaku*
800	八百 *happyaku*
1000	千 *sen*
2000	二千 *nisen*
3000	三千 *sanzen*
10000	一万 *ichiman*
100000	十万 *jûman*
1000000	百万 *hyakuman*
first	一番目 *ichibamme*, 最初 *saisho*
second	二番目 *nibamme*
third	三番目 *sambamme*
fourth	四番目 *yombamme*
fifth	五番目 *gobamme*
sixth	六番目 *rokubamme*
seventh	七番目 *nanabamme*
eighth	八番目 *hachibamme*
ninth	九番目 *kyûbamme*
tenth	十番目 *jûbamme*
twentieth	二十番目 *nijûbamme*

NUMBERS

20 plus 3 equals 23
20足す 3 は23
nijû tasu san wa nijûsan

20 minus 3 equals 17
20引く 3 は17
nijû hiku san wa jûnana

20 multiplied by 4 equals 80
20かける 4 は80
nijû kakeru yon wa hachijû

20 divided by 4 equals 5
20割る 4 は 5
nijû waru yon wa go

Counters

As mentioned above, you will be understood even if you do not use these counters. However, it is useful to be familiar with the most common for understanding. The pronunciation may change when some counters are combined with certain numbers, but don't worry too much about this, as you should still be understood.

枚 *mai*   flat objects (pieces of paper etc)
個 *ko*   small to medium-sized objects (apples etc)
本 *hon/pon/bon*   long thin objects (pens etc)
杯 *hai/pai*   cups/glasses full (note 一杯 *ippai* one cup/glass)
軒 *ken*   buildings
冊 *satsu*   books, magazines etc

DICTIONARY

Note that *(vt)* indicates that a verb is transitive, ie that it takes an object, and *(vi)* that it is intransitive, ie does not take an object. For example, **to change money** is transitive; **the town has changed** is intransitive.

A

able: to be able to ... ことができる (verb) + *koto ga dekiru* (see grammar)

about *(concerning)*... について ... *ni tsuite*; *(approximately)* 大体 *daitai*; **to be about to do** ... よ うとしている (verb stem) + *yô to shite iru* (see grammar)

above ... の上 ... *no ue*

abroad 海外に *kaigai ni*

accept 受け入れる *ukeireru*

access *(n) (entrance)* 入口 *iriguchi* **127**; *(to computer)* アクセス *akusesu*

access *(v)* 接続する *setsuzoku suru*

accident 事故 *jiko* **34**, **125**

accommodation 宿泊施設 *shukuhaku shisetsu*

across ... を越えて ... *o koete*, 横切って *yokogitte*

adaptor アダプター *adaputâ*

address 住所 *jûsho*

admission 入場料 *nyûjôryô*

advance: in advance 前もって *mae motte*

advice アドバイス *adobaisu*; **to ask someone's advice** アドバイスを求める *adobaisu o motomeru*

advise アドバイスする *adobaisu suru*

aeroplane 飛行機 *hikôki*

after ... の後 ... *no ato*

afternoon 午後 *gogo*

again もう一度 *mô ichi do*

against ... に対して ... *ni taishite*

age 年 *toshi*, 年齢 *nenrê*

air 空気 *kûki*

air conditioning エアコン *eakon*

airline 航空会社 *kôkû gaisha*

airmail 航空便 *kôkûbin*

airport 空港 *kûkô*

alarm clock 目覚し時計 *mezamashi dokê*

alcohol アルコール *arukôru*, 酒 *sake*

alive *(living)* 生きている *ikite iru*; *(busy)* 活発な *kappatsu na*

all 全部 *zembu*, 全て *subete*; **all day** 一日中 *ichi nichi jû*; **all week** 一週間毎日 *isshûkan mai nichi*; **all the better** ずっといい *zutto î*; **all the time** いつも *itsumo*; **all inclusive** 全込み *zenkomi*; **all right** 大丈夫 *daijôbu*

allergic アレルギー *arerugî* **51**, **121**,**123**

almost ほとんど *hotondo*

already もう *mô*, すでに *sude ni*

also ... も ... *mo*

although ... だけれど ... *da keredo*

always いつも *itsumo*

ambulance 救急車 *kyûkyûsha* **119**

American (n) アメリカ人 amerikajin

American (adj) アメリカの amerika no

among … の間に … no aida ni

anaesthetic 麻酔 masui

and (connecting sentences) そして soshite; (connecting nouns) と to

animal アニメ anime

animation 動物 dôbutsu

ankle 足首 ashikubi

anniversary 記念日 kinembi

another 他の hoka no

answer (n) 答 kotae

answer (v) 答える kotaeru

answering machine 留守番電話 rusuban denwa

ant アリ ari

antibiotics 抗生物質 kôsê busshitsu

anybody, anyone 誰か dare ka; (with negative) 誰も dare mo, 誰でも dare de mo

anything 何か nani ka, 何も nani mo; (with negative) 何でも nan de mo

anyway ともかく tomokaku

appendicitis 盲腸 (炎) môchô(en)

appointment 約束 yakusoku, 予約 yoyaku; **to make an appointment** 予約する yoyaku suru 118; **to have an appointment with** … と予約してある … to yoyaku shite aru 119

April 四月 shigatsu

area (place) 地域 chi-iki; (measurement) 面積 menseki; **in the area** のあたりで no atari de

arm 腕 ude

around 周りに mawari ni

arrange 手配する tehai suru; **to arrange to meet** 会う約束をす る au yakusoku o suru

arrival 到着 tôchaku

arrive 着く tsuku, 到着する tôchaku suru

art 芸術 gêjutsu

artist 芸術家 gêjutsuka

as として toshite; **as soon as possible** できるだけ早く dekiru dake hayaku; **as soon as** … とす ぐに … to sugu ni; **as well as** … だけでなく … dake de naku

ashtray 灰皿 haizara 49

ask 尋ねる tazuneru, 聞く kiku; **to ask a question** 質問する shitsumon suru

aspirin アスピリン asupirin

asthma 喘息 zensoku

at … で de, に … ni (see grammar)

attack (v) 襲う osou 126

August 八月 hachigatsu

aunt (one's own) おば oba; (someone else's) おばさん oba-san

autumn 秋 aki

available 利用できる riyô dekiru

away 離れた hanareta; **10 km away** 10キロ離れている jikkiro hanarete iru

B

baby 赤ん坊 akambô, 赤ちゃん akachan

baby's bottle 哺乳瓶 honyûbin

back (behind) 後ろ ushiro; (of body) 背中 senaka; **at the back of** … の後ろに … no ushiro ni

backpack バックパック bakkupakku

bad よくない yokunai, 悪い warui; **it's not bad** まあまあ mâmâ

bag かばん kaban, バッグ baggu

baggage 荷物 nimotsu
bake 焼く yaku
baker's パン屋 pan ya
balcony バルコニー barukonî
bandage 包帯 hôtai
bank 銀行 ginkô 104
banknote 紙幣 shihê, お札 osatsu
bar バー bâ
barbecue バーベキュー bâbekyû
bath 風呂 furo, バス basu; to
  have a bath 風呂に入る furo
  ni hairu
bathroom 風呂場 furoba
bath towel バスタオル basu
  taoru
battery 電池 denchi
be (people, animals) いる iru;
  (things) ある aru, だ da (see
  grammar)
beach 海岸 kaigan, 浜辺 hamabe
bear 熊 kuma
beard あごひげ agohige
beautiful 美しい utsukushî, きれ
  い kirê
because なぜなら naze nara, ...
  から ... kara; because of のた
  め no tame
bed ベッド beddo
bee 蜂 hachi
before ... の前に ... no mae ni,
  以前 izen
begin (vt) 始める hajimeru; (vi) 始
  まる hajimaru
beginner 初心者 shoshinsha
beginning 始め hajime; at the
  beginning 最初 saisho
behind ... の後ろに ... no ushiro
  ni
believe 信じる shinjiru
below ... の下 ... no shita
beside ... の隣 ... no tonari
best 一番よい ichi ban yoi; the

best 一番よいもの ichi ban yoi
  mono
better よりよい yori yoi; to get
  better よくなる yoku naru; it's
  better not to go, you'd better
  not go 行かないほうがいい
  ikanai hô ga î (see grammar)
between ... の間 ... no aida
bicycle 自転車 jitensha
bicycle pump 空気入れ kûki ire
big 大きい ôkî
bike 自転車 jitensha
bill 勘定 kanjô 55
bin ゴミ箱 gomi bako
binoculars 双眼鏡 sôgankyô
bird 鳥 tori
birthday 誕生日 tanjôbi
bit: a bit 少し sukoshi
bite (n) (from dog) かみ傷 kamikizu;
  (from insect) 虫刺され mushi
  sasare
bite (v) かむ kamu
black (n) 黒 kuro
black (adj) 黒い kuroi
blackout (electric) 停電 têden;
  (loss of consciousness) 意識不明
  ishiki fumê
blanket 毛布 môfu
bleed 出血する shukketsu suru
blind (n) ブラインド buraindo
blind (adj) 目の不自由な me no
  fujiyû na
blister まめ mame
blonde 金髪 kimpatsu
blood 血 chi, 血液 ketsueki
blood pressure 血圧 ketsuatsu
blue (n) 青 ao
blue (adj) 青い aoi
board (v) 乗る noru 28
boarding (of boat) 乗船 jôsen; (of
  plane) 搭乗 tôjô
boat ボート bôto, 船 fune

body 体 *karada*
book (n) 本 *hon*; **book of tickets** 回数券 *kaisûken*
book (v) 予約する *yoyaku suru* **26**
bookshop 本屋 *hon ya*
boot (footwear) ブーツ *bûtsu*; (of car) トランク *toranku*
boring つまらない *tsumaranai*
borrow 借りる *kariru*
botanical garden 植物園 *shokubutsuen*
both 両方 *ryô hô*; **both of us** 二人とも *futari tomo*
bottle びん *bin*
bottle opener 栓抜き *sennuki*
bottom 底 *soko*; **at the bottom** 最後に *saigo ni*; **at the bottom of** ... の奥 ... *no oku*
bowl ボウル *bôru*
bra ブラ *bura*
brake (n) ブレーキ *burêki*
brake (v) ブレーキをかける *burêki o kakeru*
bread パン *pan*
break (object) 壊す *kowasu*; (bone) 骨折する *kossetsu suru*; **to break one's leg** 足を折る *ashi o oru*
break down 故障する *koshô suru* **126**
breakdown (in car) 故障 *koshô*
breakdown service 故障修理 *koshô shûri*
breakfast 朝食 *chôshoku*, 朝ごはん *asagohan* **42**; **to have breakfast** 朝食を食べる *chôshoku o taberu*, 朝ごはんを食べる *asagohan o taberu*
bridge 橋 *hashi*; (game) ブリッジ *burijji*
bring (things) 持って来る *motte kuru*; (people) 連れて来る *tsurete kuru*

brochure パンフレット *pamfuretto*
broken (thing) 壊れた *kowareta*; (bone) 折れた *oreta*, 骨折した *kossetu shita*
bronchitis 気管支炎 *kikanshien*
brother (elder – one's own) 兄 *ani*; (– someone else's) お兄さん *onî-san*; (younger – one's own) 弟 *otôto*; (– someone else's) 弟さん *otôto-san*
brown (n) 茶色 *chairo*
brown (adj) 茶色い *chairoi*
brush ブラシ *burashi*
buggy (for baby) ベビーカー *bebîkâ*
build 建てる *tateru*
building 建物 *tatemono*
bump (v) こぶ *kobu*
bumper バンパー *bampâ*
buoy ブイ *bui*
burn (n) やけど *yakedo*
burn (vi) 焼く *yaku*; (vt) 焼ける *yakeru*; **to burn oneself** やけどする *yakedo suru*
burst (v) 爆発する *bakuhatsu suru*, はじける *hajikeru*
bus バス *basu* **32**
business card 名刺 *mêshi*
business class ビジネスクラス *bijinesu kurasu*
business trip 出張 *shutchô*
bus route バス路線 *basu rosen*
bus station バスターミナル *basu tâminaru*, バスセンター *basu sentâ*
bus stop バス停 *basu tê* **32**
busy (person) 忙しい *isogashî*; (place) 混んでいる *konde iru*, にぎやかな *nigiyaka na*
but でも *demo*
butcher's 肉屋 *nikuya*
buy 買う *kau* **26**, **91**
by (nearby) ... のそばで ... *no*

soba de; **by car** 車で kuruma de
bye! バイバイ baibai

C

café 喫茶店 kissaten
call (n) 電話 denwa
call (v) 呼ぶ yobu; (on phone) 電話
　する denwa suru **115**
call back 折り返し電話する
　orikaeshi denwa suru, かけなおす
　kakenaosu **115**
camcorder ビデオカメラ bideo
　kamera
camera カメラ kamera
camper キャンパー kyampâ
camping キャンプ kyampu; **to go
　camping** キャンプする kyampu
　suru
camping stove キャンプ用コン
　ロ kyampu yô konro
campsite キャンプ場 kyampu
　jô **46**
can (n) カン kan
can (v) できる dekiru; **I can't** でき
　ない dekinai
cancel キャンセルする kanseru
　suru, 取り消す torikesu
candle ろうそく rôsoku
can opener 缶切り kankiri
car 車 kuruma, 自動車 jidôsha
caravan キャンピングカー
　kyampingu kâ
card (playing card) トランプ
　torampu; (credit card etc) カー
　ド kâdo
car park 駐車場 chûsha jô
carry 運ぶ hakobu
cartoon 漫画 manga
case: in case of … の場合 …
　no bâi
cash 現金 genkin; **to pay cash** 現

金で払う genkin de harau
cashpoint 現金自動支払機 genkin
　jidô shiharai ki, ＡＴＭ êtîemu **104,
　105**
castle 城 shiro
cat 猫 neko
catch 捕まえる tsukamaeru
CD CD shîdî
cemetery 墓地 bochi
centimetre センチ(メートル)
　senchi(mêtoru)
centre 中心 chûshin, センター
　sentâ **42**
century 世紀 sêki
chair 椅子 isu
chairlift リフト rifuto
change (n) 変更 henkô; (money) お
　つり otsuri
change (vi) 変わる kawaru; (vt)
　変える kaeru; (money) 両替す
　る ryôgae suru
changing room 試着室 shichaku
　shitsu
channel チャンネル channeru
chapel 礼拝堂 rêhaidô
charge (n) (money) 料金 ryôkin
charge (v) 代金を請求する daikin
　o sêkyû suru; (battery) 充電する
　jûden suru
cheap 安い yasui
check 調べる shiraberu, 確かめる
　tashikameru
check in チェックインする
　chekkuin suru
check-in チェックイン chekkuin
　28
checkout チェックアウト chekku
　auto
cheers! 乾杯 kampai!
cheese チーズ chîzu
chemist's 薬屋 kusuriya, 薬局
　yakkyoku

chest 胸 *mune*

chest measurement 胸囲 *kyôi*

child 子供 *kodomo*

chilly *(wind)* ちょっと冷たい *chotto tsumetai; (weather)* 肌寒い *hadazamui*

chimney 煙突 *entotsu*

chin あご *ago*

China 中国 *chûgoku*

Chinese *(n) (person)* 中国人 *chûgokujin; (language)* 中国語 *chûgokugo*

Chinese *(adj)* 中国の *chûgoku no*

chips フライドポテト *furaido poteto*

chocolate チョコレート *chokorêto*

chopsticks はし *hashi*

church 教会 *kyôkai*

cigar 葉巻 *hamaki*

cigarette タバコ *tabako*

cinema 映画館 *êgakan*

circus サーカス *sâkasu*

city 都市 *toshi*

clean *(adj)* きれいな *kirê na*

clean *(v)* 掃除する *sôji suru*

cliff がけ *gake*

climate 気候 *kikô*

climbing 登山 *tozan*

cloakroom 携帯品一時預かり所 *kêtaihin ichiji azukarijo*

close *(vt)* 閉める *shimeru; (vi)* 閉まる *shimaru*

closed *(shop, restaurant)* 閉店 *hêten*, 準備中 *jumbi chû; (museum, gallery)* 閉館 *hêkan*

closing time 閉店時間 *hêten jikan*, 閉館時間 *hêkan jikan*

clothes 服 *fuku*

cloud 雲 *kumo*

cloudy くもり *kumori*

clutch *(in car)* クラッチ *kuratchi*

coach 長距離バス *chôkyôri basu* **32**

coast 海岸 *kaigan*

coathanger ハンガー *hangâ*

cockroach ゴキブリ *gokiburi*

coffee コーヒー *kôhî*

coin 硬貨 *kôka*, 小銭 *kozeni*

Coke® コーラ *kôra*

cold *(n)* 風邪 *kaze;* to have a cold 風邪をひいている *kaze o hîte iru*

cold *(adj)* 寒い *samui;* it's/I'm cold 寒い(です) *samui (desu)*

collection コレクション *korekushon*

colour 色 *iro* **97**

comb 櫛 *kushi*

come 来る *kuru*

come back 戻って来る *modotte kuru*

come in 入る *hairu*

come out 出る *deru*

comfortable 快適な *kaiteki na*

company *(business)* 会社 *kaisha*

complain 文句を言う *monku o yû*, 苦情を言う *kujô o yû*

comprehensive insurance 総合自動車保険 *sôgô jidôsha hoken*

computer コンピュータ *kompyûta*

concert コンサート *konsâto* **74**

concert hall コンサートホール *konsâto hôru*

concession *(discount)* （老人、学生の）割引 *(rôjin, gakusê no) waribiki* **26**

conditioner *(for hair)* リンス *rinsu*

condom コンドーム *kondômu*

confirm 確認する *kakunin suru*

connection 接続 *setsuzoku; (in transport)* 乗り換え *norikae* **28**

constipated 便秘 *bempi*

consulate 領事館 *ryôjikan* **125**

consumer tax 消費税 *shôhizê*

contact (n) (connection) 連絡 renraku

contact (v) 連絡する renraku suru **113**

contact lenses コンタクト(レンズ) kontakuto (renzu)

contagious: to be contagious 伝染する densen suru

contraceptive 避妊 hinin

cook (v) 料理する ryôri suru

cooked 調理された chôri sareta

cooking クッキング kukkingu, 料理 ryôri; **to do the cooking** 料理する ryôri suru

cool (weather) 涼しい suzushî; (thing) 冷たい tsumetai; (attractive) かっこいい kakko î; (calm) 冷静な rêsê na

corkscrew コルク抜き korukunuki

correct 正しい tadashî

cost (n) 値段 nedan

cost (v) (金額が)かかる (kingaku ga) kakaru

cotton 綿 men

cotton bud 綿棒 membô

cotton wool 脱脂綿 dasshimen

cough (n) せき seki; **to have a cough** せきをする seki o suru

cough (v) せきをする seki o suru

count 数える kazoeru

country 国 kuni

countryside いなか inaka

course コース kôsu; **of course** もちろん mochiron

cover (n) カバー kabâ

cover (v) 覆う ôu

credit card クレジットカード kurejitto kâdo **40**, **50**, **105**, **126**

cross (n) 十文字 jûmonji; (mark) バツ batsu

cross (v) 横切る yokogiru, 渡る wataru

crowded 混んでいる konde iru

cruise クルーズ kurûzu

cry (n) 泣き声 nakigoe

cry (v) (weep) 泣く naku; (shout) 叫ぶ sakebu

cup カップ kappu

currency 通貨 tsûka

customs 税関 zêkan

cut (n) 切り傷 kirikizu

cut (v) 切る kiru; **to cut oneself** 切る kiru

cycle path サイクリングコース saikuringu kôsu **88**

D

damaged 傷のついた kizu no tsuita

damp じめじめした jimejime shita

dance (n) ダンス dansu, 踊り odori

dance (v) 踊る odoru

dangerous 危ない abunai

dark 暗い kurai

date (n) 日にち hinichi; (romantic) デート dêto; **out of date** 期限切れ kigen gire

date (from) … に始まった … ni hajimatta

date of birth 生年月日 sênengappi

daughter (one's own) 娘 musume; (someone else's) 娘さん musume-san

day 日 hi/nichi; **the day after tomorrow** あさって asatte; **the day before yesterday** おととい ototoi

dead 死んだ shinda

deaf 耳の不自由な mimi no fujiyû na

dear (expensive) 高い takai

December 十二月 jûnigatsu

declare (at customs) 申告する
shinkoku suru

deep 深い fukai

deer 鹿 shika

degree 程度 têdo; (in temperature)
度 do

delay 遅延 chien, 遅れ okure

delayed 遅れた okureta

delicatessen デリカテッセン
derikatessen

dentist 歯医者 haisha

deodorant 防臭剤 bôshûzai

department 部門 bumon; (in shop)
売り場 uriba

department store デパート
depâto

departure 出発 shuppatsu

deposit 手付金 tetsukekin, 保証
金 hoshôkin

dessert デザート dezâto **51**

develop 発達する hattatsu suru

diabetes 糖尿病 tônyôbyô

dialling code 局番 kyoku ban

diarrhoea 下痢 geri; **to have
diarrhoea** 下痢する geri suru

die 死ぬ shinu

diesel ディーゼル dîzeru

diet ダイエット daietto; **to be on
a diet** ダイエットをしている
daietto o shite iru

different (from) … と違う …
to chigau

difficult 難しい muzukashî

digital camera デジタルカメラ
dejitaru kamera, デジカメ dejikame

dinner 夕食 yûshoku, 夕飯 yûhan,
晩ご飯 bangohan; **to have dinner**
夕飯を食べる yûhan o taberu

direct (adj) 直接の chokusetsu no

direction 方向 hôkô; **to have a
bad sense of direction** 方向オ
ンチだ hôkô onchi da

directory enquiries 番号案内
bangô annai

dirty (adj) 汚い kitanai

disabled 体の不自由な karada no
fujiyû na **127**

disappointed がっかりした
gakkari shita

disaster 災害 saigai

disco ディスコ disuko

discount 割引 waribiki, ディス
カウント dis kaunto; **to give
someone a discount** 割り引い
てあげる waribîte ageru

discount fare 割引運賃 waribiki
unchin

dish (plate) 皿 sara; (food) 料理
ryôri; **dish of the day** 本日のお奨
め honjitsu no osusume

dishes: to do the dishes 皿洗い
をする sara arai o suru

disinfect 消毒する shôdoku suru

disposable 使い捨て tsukaisute

disturb 邪魔をする jama o suru;
do not disturb (on sign) 起こ
さないでください okosanaide
kudasai

diving: to go diving ダイビング
をする daibingu o suru

do する suru

doctor 医者 isha **118**

dog 犬 inu

door ドア doa, 戸 to

downstairs 階下 kaika

draught beer 生ビール nama
bîru

dress (n) ドレス doresu

dress: to get dressed 服を着る
fuku o kiru

dressing (for wound) 傷の手当用
品 kizu no teate yôhin

drink (n) 飲み物 nomimono; **to go
for a drink** 飲みに行く nomi ni

150

iku **48**, **71**; to have a drink 飲
む nomu

drink (v) 飲む nomu

drinking water 飲み水 nomi mizu

drive (n) **to go for a drive** ドラ
イブする doraibu suru

drive (v) 運転する unten suru

driving licence 運転免許 unten
menkyo

drown (v) おぼれる oboreru

drugs (medicinal) 薬 kusuri; (illegal)
麻薬 mayaku

drunk 酔っ払った yopparatta

dry (adj) 乾いた kawaita

dry (vt) 乾かす kawakasu; (vi) 乾
く kawaku

dry cleaner's クリーニング屋
kurîningu ya

during … の間 … no aida

dustbin ごみ箱 gomi bako

E

each それぞれの sorezore no;
each one それぞれ sorezore

ear 耳 mimi

early (adj) 早い hayai

early (adv) 早く hayaku

earplug 耳栓 mimi sen

earrings イアリング iaringu; (for
pierced ears) ピアス piasu

earth (world) 地球 chikyû; (land) 地
面 jimen

earthquake 地震 jishin

east 東 higashi; **in the east** 東に
higashi ni; **(to the) east of** … の
東 … no higashi

easy やさしい yasashî, 簡単な
kantan na

eat 食べる taberu **48**

economy class エコノミークラ
ス ekonomî kurasu

egg 卵 tamago

electric 電気の denki no

electricity 電気 denki

electricity meter 電気のメータ
ー denki no mêtâ

electric shaver 電気かみそり
denki kamisori

e-mail Eメールî-mêru, 電子メー
ル denshi mêru

e-mail address メールアドレス
mêru adoresu

embassy 大使館 taishikan **125**

emergency 緊急 kinkyû; **in an
emergency** 非常の際 hijô no sai

emergency exit 非常口 hijô guchi

empty 空 kara

end 終わり owari; **at the end of**
…の最後に … no saigo ni; **at the
end of the street** 道の突き当た
り michi no tsukiatari

engaged (in use) 使用中 shiyô chû;
(couple) 婚約している kon'yaku
shite iru

engine エンジン enjin

England イングランド ingurando

English (n) (language) 英語 êgo
125; (people) イングランド人
ingurandojin

English (adj) イングランドの
ingurando no

enjoy 楽しむ tanoshimu; **to enjoy
oneself** 楽しむ tanoshimu

enough 十分 jûbun; **that's
enough** もう結構です mô kekkô
desu

entrance 入口 iriguchi

envelope 封筒 fûtô

epileptic てんかん tenkan

espresso エスプレッソ esupuresso

Europe ヨーロッパ yôroppa

European (n) ヨーロッパの人
yôroppa no hito

European (adj) ヨーロッパの yôroppa no

evening 夕方 yûgata, 夜 yoru; **in the evening** 夕方 yûgata

every 全ての subete no; **every day** 毎日 mai nichi

everybody, everyone みんな minna

everywhere どこでも doko demo

except … を除いて … o nozoite

excess: excess baggage 重量 オーバーの荷物 jûryô ôbâ no nimotsu

exchange (v) (one thing for another) 交換する kôkan suru; (money) 両替する ryôgae suru

exchange rate 両替率 ryôgae ritsu

excuse (n) 言い訳 îwake

excuse (v) 許す yurusu; **excuse me** すみません sumimasen

exhausted くたくた kutakuta

exhaust pipe 排気管 haiki kan

exhibition 展覧会 tenrankai 79

exit 出口 deguchi

expensive 高い takai

expiry date 有効期限 yûkô kigen

express train 急行(列車) kyûkô (ressha)

extra 余分の yobun no

eye 目 me

eye drops 目薬 megusuri

F

face 顔 kao

facecloth 洗面用タオル semmen yô taoru

fact 事実 jijitsu; **in fact** 実は jitsu wa

faint (v) 失神する shisshin suru

fall (v) 落ちる ochiru; **to fall asleep** 眠りに落ちる nemuri ni

ochiru; **to fall ill** 病気になる byôki ni naru

family 家族 kazoku

fan (object) 扇子 sensu

far 遠い tôi; **far from** … から遠い … kara tôi

fare 運賃 unchin

fast 速い hayai

fast-food restaurant ファースト フードの店 fâsuto fûdo no mise

fat (adj) 太っている futotte iru

fat (n) 脂肪 shibô

father (one's own) 父 chichi; (someone else's) お父さん otô-san

favour: to ask someone a favour お願いする onegai suru; **can you do me a favour?** お願 いしたいんですが onegai shitai n desu ga

favourite 好物 kôbutsu, とても好 きなもの totemo suki na mono

fax ファックス fakkusu

February 二月 nigatsu

fed up: to be fed up with … に 飽き飽きする … ni akiaki suru

feel 感じる kanjiru; **to feel good/bad** 気持ちがいい・悪い kimochi ga îwarui

feeling 感じ kanji; (sense) 感覚 kankaku

ferry フェリー ferî

festival 祭り matsuri, フェスティ バル fesutibaru

fetch: to go and fetch someone を連れて来る o tsurete kuru; **to go and fetch something** 持って 来る motte kuru

fever 熱 netsu; **to have a fever** 熱 がある netsu ga aru

few ほとんどない hotondo nai

fiancé フィアンセ fianse, 婚約者 kon'yakusha

fiancée フィアンセ *fianse*, 婚約者 *kon'yakusha*
fight けんか *kenka*
fill いっぱいにする *ippai ni suru*
fill in 記入する *kinyû suru*
fill up いっぱいにする *ippai ni suru*; **to fill up with petrol** 満タンにする *man tan ni suru*
filling (in tooth) 詰め物 *tsumemono*
film (for camera) フィルム *firumu*, フイルム *fuirumu* **101**; (movie) 映画 *êga*
finally ついに *tsui ni*
find 見つける *mitsukeru*
fine (n) 罰金 *bakkin*
fine (adj) (good) 立派な *rippa na*; (weather) 晴れている *harete iru*; **I'm fine** 大丈夫 *daijôbu*
finger 指 *yubi*
finish (v) 終わる *owaru*
fire 火 *hi*; **fire!** 火事だ *kaji da!*
fire brigade 消防隊 *shôbôtai*
fireworks 花火 *hanabi*
first 最初 *saisho*; **first (of all)** まず最初に *mazu saisho ni*
first floor 二階 *ni kai*
first name 名前 *namae*, 名 *na*
fish (n) 魚 *sakana*
fishmonger's, fish shop 魚屋 *sakana ya*
fitting room 試着室 *shichaku shitsu*
fizzy 炭酸入りの *tansan iri no*
flash フラッシュ *furasshu*
flask 魔法瓶 *mahôbin*
flat (adj) 平らな *taira na*; **flat tyre** パンク *panku*
flat (n) アパート *apâto*
flavour 味 *aji*
flight 便 *bin*
floor 床 *yuka*; **on the floor** 床の上に *yuka no ue ni*

flower 花 *hana*
flu インフルエンザ *infuruenza*
fly (n) ハエ *hae*
fly (v) 飛ぶ *tobu*
food 食べ物 *tabemono* **94**
food poisoning 食中毒 *shoku chûdoku*
foot 足 *ashi*
forbidden 禁止された *kinshi sareta*
forecast 予報 *yohô*
forehead 額 *hitai*
foreign 外国の *gaikoku no*
foreigner 外国人 *gaikokujin*
forest 森 *mori*
fork フォーク *fôku*
former 前の *mae no*
forward (adj) 前に *mae ni*
fracture 骨折 *kossetsu*
fragile われもの *waremono*
France フランス *furansu*
free 自由 *jiyû*; (of charge) 無料 *muryô*; (time) 暇な *hima na*
freezer 冷凍庫 *rêtôko*
Friday 金曜日 *kin'yôbî*
fridge 冷蔵庫 *rêzôko*
fried 揚げた *ageta*
friend 友達 *tomodachi*, 友人 *yûjin*
from … から … *kara*; **from … to …** … から … まで … *kara … made*
front 前 *mae*; **in front of** … の前 … *no mae*
fry 揚げる *ageru*
frying pan フライパン *furaipan*
full いっぱい *ippai*; **full of** … でいっぱい … *de ippai*
full board 三食付 *san shoku tsuki*
full fare, full price 正規料金 *sêki ryôkin*
funfair 遊園地 *yûenchi*
fuse ヒューズ *hyûzu*

gallery 美術館 bijutsukan

game ゲーム gêmu; (match) 試合 shiai **89**

garage (for repairs) 修理工場 shûri kôjô **34**

garden 庭 niwa

gas ガス gasu

gas cylinder (キャンプ用) ガスボンベ (kyampu yô) gasu bombe

gastric flu 胃腸障害を起こすインフルエンザ ichô shôgai o okosu infuruenza

gate 門 mon

gauze ガーゼ gâze

gay (adj) 同性愛の dôsêai no

gay (n) 同性愛者 dôsêaisha

gearbox ギアボックス giabokkusu

general 一般的 ippanteki

gents' (toilet) 男性用トイレ dansê yô toire

Germany ドイツ doitsu

get 手に入れる te ni ireru

get off 降りる oriru **32**

get up 起きる okiru

gift wrap プレゼント用の包装 purezento yô no hôsô

girl 女の子 onna no ko, 少女 shôjo

girlfriend ガールフレンド gârufurendo

give 与える ataeru, あげる ageru

give back 返す kaesu

glass (substance) ガラス garasu; (for drinking) コップ koppu; **a glass of water/of wine** 水・ワインを一杯 mizu/wain o ippai

glasses メガネ megane

gluten-free グルテンなし guruten nashi

go 行く iku; **to go to Tokyo/Japan** 東京・日本に行く tôkyô/nihon ni iku; **we're going home tomorrow** 明日帰る ashita kaeru

go away 立ち去る tachisaru

go in (中に) 入る (naka ni) hairu

go out 出かける dekakeru

go with (someone) … と一緒に行く … to issho ni iku; (food, clothes) … とよく合う … to yoku au

golf ゴルフ gorufu

golf course ゴルフコース gorufu kôsu

good いいî, よい yoi; **good morning** おはようございます ohayô gozaimasu; **good afternoon** こんにちは konnichiwa; **good evening** こんばんは kombanwa

goodbye さようなら sayônara

good night おやすみなさい oyasumi nasai

goods 商品 shôhin

grams グラム guramu **95**

grandchild (one's own) 孫 mago; (someone else's) お孫さん omago-san

grass 草 kusa

great! すごい！ sugoi!

Great Britain 英国 êkoku, イギリス igirisu

green (n) 緑 midori

green (adj) 緑の midori no

green light 青信号 ao shingô

grey (n) グレイ gurê

grey (adj) グレの gurê no

ground 地面 jimen; **on the ground** 地面に jimen ni

ground floor 一階 ikkai

ground sheet グランドシート gurando shîto

grow (vi) 成長する sêchô suru

guarantee 保証 hoshô

guest (お)客 *(o)kyaku*
guide (n) ガイド *gaido* **73**
guidebook ガイドブック *gaidobukku*
guided tour ガイド付き見学コース *gaido tsuki kengaku kôsu*
gynaecologist 婦人科医 *fujinka i*

H

hail (n) あられ *arare*, ひょう *hyô*
hail (v) ひょうが降る *hyô ga furu*
hair (髪の)毛 *(kami no) ke*
hairdresser's 美容院 *biyôin*
hairdrier ドライヤー *doraiyâ*
half 半分 *hambun*; **half an hour** 三十分 *sanjippun*
half-board 二食付き *ni shoku tsuki*
hand 手 *te*
handbag ハンドバッグ *handobaggu*
handbrake サイドブレーキ *saido burêki*
handicapped 障害のある *shôgai no aru*
handkerchief ハンカチ *hankachi*
hand luggage 手荷物 *tenimotsu* **28**
hand-made 手作り *tezukuri*
hangover 二日酔い *futsukayoi*
happen 起きる *okiru*
happy 幸せな *shiawase na*, うれしい *ureshî*
hard (not soft) 硬い *katai*; (difficult) 難しい *muzukashî*
hat 帽子 *bôshi*
hate 大嫌いだ *dai kirai da*
have 持っている *motte iru*
have to ... なければならない ... *nakereba naranai*; **I have to go** 行かなければならない *ikanakereba naranai* (see grammar)

hay fever 花粉症 *kafunshô*
he 彼 *kare*
head 頭 *atama*
headache 頭痛 *zutsû*; **to have a headache** 頭が痛い *atama ga itai*
headlight ヘッドライト *heddoraito*
health 健康 *kenkô*
hear 聞く *kiku*
heart 心臓 *shinzô*
heart attack 心臓まひ *shinzô mahi*
heat 熱 *netsu*
heating 暖房 *dambô*
heavy 重い *omoi*
height (of person) 身長 *shinchô*; (of thing) 高さ *takasa*
hello こんにちは *konnichiwa*
helmet ヘルメット *herumetto*
help (n) 助け *tasuke*; **to call for help** 助けを求める *tasuke o motomeru*; **help!** 助けて *tasukete!*
help (v) (rescue) 助ける *tasukeru*; (assist) 手伝う *tetsudau*
her 彼女 *kanojo*
herbal tea ハーブティー *hâbu tî*
hi-fi ハイファイ *haifai*
high 高い *takai*
high blood pressure 高血圧 *kôketsuatsu*
high tide 満潮 *manchô*
hiking ハイキング *haikingu*; **to go hiking** ハイキングをする *haikingu o suru* **86**
hill 丘 *oka*
hill-walking 山歩き *yama aruki*; **to go hill-walking** 山歩きをする *yama aruki o suru*
hip 腰 *koshi*, ヒップ *hippu*
hire (n) 賃借り *chingari*, レンタル *rentaru*
hire (v) 賃借りする *chingari suru*,

レンタルする rentaru suru **35**, **84**

hitchhike ヒッチハイクする hitchhaiku suru

hitchhiking ヒッチハイク hitchhaiku

hold (v) つかんでいる tsukande iru

hold on! (on the phone) 少々、お待ちください shôshô omachi kudasai

holiday(s) 休み yasumi, 休暇 kyûka; **on holiday** 休暇を取って kyûka o totte **19**

home 家 ie/uchi; **to go home** 帰宅する kitaku suru, (家に)帰る (ie ni) kaeru

homosexual (adj) 同性愛の dôsêai no

homosexual (n) (male) ホモ homo; (female) レズ rezu

honest 正直な shôjiki na

honeymoon 新婚旅行 shinkon ryokô

Hong Kong 香港 honkon

horse 馬 uma

hospital 病院 byôin

hot あつい atsui; **it's hot** あつい（です）atsui (desu); **hot drink** 温かい飲み物 atakai nomimono

hot chocolate ココア kokoa

hot spring 温泉 onsen

hotel ホテル hoteru

hour 時間 jikan; **an hour and a half** 一時間半 ichi jikan han

house 家 ie/uchi

housework 家事 kaji; **to do the housework** 家事をする kaji o suru

how どう dô; **how are you?** お元気ですか ogenki desu ka?

humour ユーモア yûmoa

hungry: to be hungry おなかが空いている onaka ga suite iru, おなかが減っている onaka ga hette iru

hurry: to be in a hurry 急いでいる isoide iru; **hurry up!** 急いで！isoide!, 急げ！isoge!

hurt: it hurts 痛い itai **120**; **my head hurts** 頭が痛い atama ga itai

husband (one's own) 夫 otto, 主人 shujin; (someone else's) ご主人 goshujin

I

I 私 watashi; **I'm English** イングランド人です ingurandojin desu; **I'm 22 (years old)** 22歳です nijûni sai desu

ice 氷 kôri

ice-cream アイスクリーム aisukurîmu

ice cube 角氷 kakugôri

identity card 身分証明書 mibunshômêsho

if もし moshi

ill 病気の byôki (no + n)

illness 病気 byôki

important 大切な taisetsu na, 大事な daiji na

in で de, に ni (see grammar); **in England/Japan** イングランドで・日本で ingurando de/nihon de; **in the 19th century** 十九世紀に jûkyû sêki ni; **in an hour** 一時間後に ichi jikan go ni

incense 香 kô

included 含まれた fukumareta **42**, **45**, **55**

independent 独立した dokuritsu shita

indicator *(on car)* 方向指示器 *hôkô shijiki*

infection 感染 *kansen*, 伝染 *densen*

information 情報 *jôhô* **78**

injection 注射 *chûsha*

injured けがをした *kega o shita*

insect 虫 *mushi*

insecticide 殺虫剤 *satchûzai*

inside 内側 *uchigawa*, の中で *no naka*, の中で *de no naki ni (see grammar)*

insomnia 不眠症 *fuminshô*

instant coffee インスタントコーヒー *insutanto kôhî*

instead その代わりに *sono kawari ni*; **instead of …** の代わりに … *no kawari ni*

insurance 保険 *hoken*

intend to … ・つもり *(verb +)* *tsumori*; **we intend to go to Nikko** 日光に行くつもりです *nikkô ni iku tsumori desu*

international 国際的な *kokusaiteki na*

international money order 国際為替 *kokusai kawase*

Internet インターネット *intânetto*

Internet café インターネットカフェ *intânetto kafe* **110**

invite 招く *maneku*

Ireland アイルランド *airurando*

Irish *(adj)* アイルランドの *airurando no*; **Irish person** アイルランド人 *airurando jin*

iron *(n) (for clothes)* アイロン *airon*

iron *(v)* アイロンをかける *airon o kakeru*

island 島 *shima*

it それ *sore*

itchy かゆい *kayui*

J

jacket 上着 *uwagi*, ジャケット *jaketto*

January 一月 *ichigatsu*

Japan 日本 *nihon/nippon*

Japanese *(person)* 日本人 *nihonjin*; *(language)* 日本語 *nihongo*

Japanese *(adj)* 日本の *nihon no*

jetlag 時差ぼけ *jisaboke*

jeweller's 宝石店 *hôseki ten*

jewellery 宝石 *hôseki*

job 仕事 *shigoto*

jogging ジョギング *jogingu*

journey 旅 *tabi*, 旅行 *ryokô*

jug 水差し *mizusashi*

juice ジュース *jûsu*

July 七月 *shichigatsu*

jumper セーター *sêtâ*

June 六月 *rokugatsu*

just *(exactly)* ちょうど *chôdo*; *(only)* … だけ … *dake*; **just before** ちょうどその前 *chôdo sono mae*; **just a little** ほんの少し *hon no sukoshi*; **just one** ひとつだけ *hitotsu dake*; **I've just arrived** 着いたばかりだ *tsuita bakari da*; **just in case** 念のために *nen no tame ni*

K

kayak カヤック *kayakku*

keep 保つ *tamotsu*

key 鍵 *kagi* **34, 42**

kidney 腎臓 *jinzô*

kill 殺す *korosu*

kilometre キロ（メートル） *kiro (mêtoru)*

kind *(n)* **what kind of?** どんな *donna?*

kind *(adj)* 親切な *shinsetsu na*

kitchen 台所 *daidokoro*
knee ひざ *hiza*
knife ナイフ *naifu*
know *(about something)* 知っている *shitte iru*; *(realize)* 分かる *wakaru*; **I don't know** 知らない *shiranai*
Korea 韓国 *kankoku*
Korean *(n) (person)* 韓国人 *kankokujin*; *(language)* 韓国語 *kankokugo*
Korean *(adj)* 韓国の *kankoku no*

L

ladies' (toilet) 女性用トイレ *josê yô toire*
lake 湖 *mizu umi*
lamp 電気スタンド *denki sutando*
landmark 目印になるもの *mejirushi ni naru mono*
landscape 景色 *keshiki*, 風景 *fûkê*
language 言語 *gengo*, 言葉 *kotoba*
laptop ノートパソコン *nôto pasokon*
last *(adj)* 最後の *saigo (no + n)*; **the last day of the exhibition** 展覧会の最後の日 *tenrankai no saigo no hi*; **last year** 去年 *kyo nen*
last *(v) (continue)* 継続する *kêzoku suru*; *(a long time)* 長持ちする *nagamochi suru*
late *(in time)* 遅い *osoi*; *(delayed)* 遅れた *okureta*
late-night opening 深夜営業 *shin'ya êgyô*
laugh *(n)* 笑い *warai*
laugh *(v)* 笑う *warau*
launderette コインランドリー *koin randorî*
lawyer 弁護士 *bengôshi*
leaflet チラシ *chirashi*

leak *(n)* 漏れ *more*
leak *(v)* 漏れる *moreru*
learn 学ぶ *manabu*, 習う *narau*
least: the least 最小の *saishô (no + n)*; **at least** 少なくとも *sukunaku tomo*
leave 離れる *hanareru*; *(depart)* 出る *deru*
left 左 *hidari*; **to the left of** … の左 … *no hidari*
left-luggage (office) 手荷物預かり所 *tenimotsu azukarijo*
leg 足 *ashi*
lend 貸す *kasu*
lens レンズ *renzu*
less より少ない *yori sukunai*
  less than … に満たない … *ni mitanai*
let *(allow)* させる *saseru*; *(house)* 賃貸する *chintai suru*
letter 手紙 *tegami*
letterbox 郵便受け *yûbin uke*
library 図書館 *toshokan*
life 人生 *jinsê*, 命 *inochi*
lift *(n)* エレベーター *erebêtâ* **42**
light *(adj) (pale)* 明るい *akarui*; *(in weight)* 軽い *karui*
light *(n)* **to switch the light on** 電気をつける *denki o tsukeru*, 明かりをつける *akari o tsukeru*
light *(v) (fire)* 火をつける *hi o tsukeru*
light bulb 電球 *denkyû*
lighter ライター *raitâ*
lighthouse 灯台 *tôdai*
like *(v)* 好きだ *suki da* **21**; **I'd like...** … がほしい … *ga hoshî*
line 線 *sen* **32**; **the line is engaged** 話し中です *hanashi chû desu*
lip 唇 *kuchibiru*
listen 聞く *kiku*

listings magazine イベント情報誌 *ibento jôhô shi*

litre リットル *rittoru*

little (adj) 小さい *chîsai*

little (adv) 少し *sukoshi*, ちょっと *chotto*

live (v) (be alive) 生きている *ikite iru*; (live somewhere) 住んでいる *sunde iru*

liver 肝臓 *kanzô*

living room 居間 *ima*

local time 現地時間 *genchi jikan*

lock (n) 鍵 *kagi*

lock (v) 鍵をかける *kagi o kakeru*

long (adj) 長い *nagai*; **a long time** 長い間 *nagai aida*; **how long …?** どのくらい … *dono kurai …*

look (see) 見る *miru*; (appear) 見える *mieru*; **to look tired** 疲れているようだ *tsukarete iru yô da*

look after 世話をする *sewa o suru*

look at … を見る *… o miru*

look for 探す *sagasu* 14, 91

look like 似ている *nite iru*

lorry トラック *torakku*

lose 失う *ushinau* 34, 126; **to get lost** 道に迷う *michi ni mayou*; **to be lost** 道に迷っている *michi ni mayotte iru* 14

lot: a lot (of) たくさん（の） *takusan (no + n)*

loud 音が大きい *oto ga ôkî*

low 低い *hikui*

low blood pressure 低血圧 *têketsuatsu*

low-fat 低脂肪 *tê shibô*

low tide 干潮 *kanchô*

luck 幸運 *kôun*; **good/bad luck** 運がいい・悪い *un ga î/warui*

lucky: to be lucky ラッキーだ *rakkî da*, 運がいい *un ga î*

luggage 荷物 *nimotsu* 28

lukewarm ぬるい *nurui*

lunch 昼食 *chûshoku*, 昼ごはん *hirugohan*; **to have lunch** 昼食・昼ごはんを食べる *chûshoku/hirugohan o taberu*

lung 肺 *hai*

luxury (n) ぜいたく *zêtaku*

luxury (adj) ぜいたくな *zêtaku na*

M

magazine 雑誌 *zasshi*

maiden name 旧姓 *kyûsê*

mail 郵便 *yûbin*

main 主な *omo na*

main course メインコース *mên kôsu*

make 作る *tsukuru*

man 男の人 *otoko no hito*, 男性 *dansê*

manage (organize) 管理する *kanri suru*; (deal with) うまく扱う *umaku atsukau*; **to manage to do something** 何とかやる *nantoka yaru*

manager マネージャー *manêjâ*

many たくさんの *takusan (no + n)*; **how many?** いくつ *ikutsu?*; **how many times …?** 何回 … *nan kai …?*

map 地図 *chizu* 14, 31, 72, 78

March 三月 *sangatsu*

marina マリーナ *marîna*

market 市場 *ichiba*

married 結婚している *kekkon shite iru*

match (for fire) マッチ *matchi*; (sport) 試合 *shiai*

material 材料 *zairyô*; (fabric) 布 *nuno*

matter: it doesn't matter いいです *î desu*

mattress マットレス *mattoresu*

May 五月 *gogatsu*

maybe 多分 *tabun*

me 私 *watashi*; **me too** 私も *watashi mo*

meal 食事 *shokuji*

mean 意味する *imi suru*; **what does ... mean?** …はどういう意味ですか? *... wa dô yû imi desu ka?*

medicine 薬 *kusuri*

medium *(size)* Mサイズ *emu saizu*; *(meat)* ミディアム *midiamu*

meet …と会う *... to au*, …に会う *... ni au* **72**

meeting 会議 *kaigi*

member メンバー *membâ*, 会員 *kai-in*

menu メニュー *menyû*

message メッセージ *messêji*, 伝言 *dengon*

meter メーター *mêtâ*

metre メートル *mêtoru*

microwave 電子レンジ *denshi renji*

midday 正午 *shôgo*

middle 真ん中 *mannaka*; **in the middle of** … の最中 *... no saichû*

midnight 真夜中 *mayonaka*

might かもしれない *kamo shirenai*; **it might rain** 雨かもしれない *ame kamo shirenai*

mind *(v)* 気にする *ki ni naru*; **I don't mind** かまわない *kamawanai*

mineral water ミネラルウォーター *mineraru wôtâ*

minister *(in government)* 大臣 *daijin*; *(in church)* 牧師 *bokushi*

minute 分 *fun/pun/bun*; **at the last minute** 土壇場になって *dotamba ni natte*

mirror 鏡 *kagami*

Miss … さん *... san*

miss し損なう *shisokonau*; **we missed the train** 列車に乗り遅れた *ressha ni noriokureta*; **there are two ... missing** … が二つ足りない *... ga futatsu tarinai*

mistake 間違い *machigai*; **to make a mistake** 間違える *machigaeru*

mobile (phone) 携帯(電話) *kêtai (denwa)* **113**

modern 近代の *kindai no*

moisturizer モイスチャークリーム *moisuchâ kurîmu*

moment 瞬間 *shunkan*; **at the moment** 今のところ *ima no tokoro*

monastery 修道院 *shûdôin*

Monday 月曜日 *getsuyôbi*

money (お)金 *(o)kane* **104**

monkey 猿 *saru*

month 月 *tsuki*

monument 記念塔 *kinentô*, 記念碑 *kinenhi*

mood 気分 *kibun*; **to be in a good/bad mood** 機嫌がいい・機嫌が悪い *kigen ga î/kigen ga warui*

moon 月 *tsuki*

moped 原付 *gentsuki*

more もっと *motto*; **more than** 以上 *ijô*; **much more, a lot more** もっとたくさん *motto takusan*; **there's no more** もうない *mô nai*

morning 朝 *asa*

mosque モスク *mosuku*

mosquito 蚊 *ka*

most: the most 最も多い *mottomo ôi*; **most people** ほとんどの人 *hotondo no hito*

mother *(one's own)* 母 *haha*; *(someone else's)* お母さん *okâ-san*

motorbike オートバイ *ôtobai*

motorway 高速道路 *kôsoku dôro*

mountain 山 *yama*

mountain bike マウンテンバイク *maunten baiku*

mountain hut 山小屋 *yama goya*

mouse *(animal)* ネズミ *nezumi*; *(for computer)* マウス *mausu*

mouth 口 *kuchi*

movie 映画 *êga*

Mr/Mrs/Ms … さん *… san*

much: how much?, how much is it?, how much does it cost? いくらですか *ikura desu ka?*

muscle 筋肉 *kinniku*

museum 博物館 *hakubutsukan*

music 音楽 *ongaku*

must *(expressing obligation)* しなければならない *shinakereba naranai*; *(expressing certainty)* … に違いない *… ni chigai nai*; **it must be 5 o'clock** 五時に違いない *go ji ni chigai nai*; **I must go** 行かなければならない *ikanakereba naranai*

myself 自分 *jibun*

N

nail *(on finger)* 爪 *tsume*

naked 裸の *hadaka (no + n)*

name 名前 *namae* **40**; **my name is** 私の名前は … です *watashi no namae wa … desu* **17**

nap 昼寝 *hirune*; **to have a nap** 昼寝をする *hirune o suru*

napkin ナプキン *napukin*

nappy オムツ *omutsu*

national holiday 祝日 *shukujitsu*

nature 自然 *shizen*

near 近く *chikaku*; **near the beach** 浜辺の近く *hamabe no chikaku*; **the nearest** 一番近い *ichi ban chikai*

necessary 必要な *hitsuyô na*

neck 首 *kubi*

need *(v)* 要る *iru*, 必要がある *hitsuyô ga aru*

neighbour 近所の人 *kinjo no hito*

neither どちらも … ない *dochira mo … nai*; **neither … nor …** … でも … でもない *… de mo … de mo nai*

nervous 神経質な *shinkêshitsu na*; *(about something)* 緊張している *kinchô shite iru*

never 決して … ない *kesshite … nai*

new 新しい *atarashî*

news ニュース *nyûsu*

newsagent 新聞販売店 *shimbun hambaiten*

newspaper 新聞 *shimbun*

newsstand 新聞売り場 *shimbun uriba*

New Year お正月 *oshôgatsu*

next 次の *tsugi no*

nice よい *yoi*, いい *î*

night 夜 *yoru* **41**

nightclub ナイトクラブ *naito kurabu*

nightdress 寝巻 *nemaki*

no いいえ *îe*; *(not any)* ひとつもない *hitotsu mo nai*; **no, thank you** いいえ、結構です *îe, kekkô desu*; **no idea** 全然分からない *zenzen wakaranai*

nobody 誰も … ない *(with negative verb) dare mo … nai*

noise 音 *oto*; **to make a noise** 音を立てる *oto o tateru*

noisy うるさい *urusai*

non-drinking water *(on sign)* 飲めません *nomemasen*

none *(nobody)* 誰も ... ない *(with negative v)* dare mo ... nai; *(nothing)* 何も ... ない *(with negative v)* nani mo ... nai

non-smoker タバコを吸わない人 *tabako o suwanai hito*

noon 正午 *shôgo*

north 北 *kita*; **in the north** 北に *kita ni*; **(to the) north of** ... の北 ... *no kita*

nose 鼻 *hana*

not ... ない *(with negative verb)* ... nai; **not yet** まだ ... ない *mada ... nai*; **not at all** 全く ... ない *mattaku ... nai*

note メモ *memo*

notebook ノート *nôto*

nothing 何も ... ない *nani mo ... nai*

novel 小説 *shôsetsu*

November 十一月 *jûichigatsu*

now 今 *ima*

nowadays 最近 *saikin*

nowhere どこにも・ない *doko ni mo ... nai*

number 番号 *bangô*; *(figure)* 数字 *sûji*

nurse 看護士 *kangoshi*

obvious 明らかな *akiraka na*

ocean 海 *umi*

o'clock ... 時 ... *ji*; **three o'clock** 三時 *san ji*

October 十月 *jûgatsu*

of ... の ... *no*

offer *(n)* 申し出 *môshide*

offer *(v)* 提供する *têkyô suru*

often よく *yoku*

oil *(for cooking)* 油 *abura*; *(for engine)* 石油 *sekiyu*

ointment 軟膏 *nankô*

OK オッケー *okkê*

old *(thing)* 古い *furui*; *(person)* 年をとった *toshi o totta*; **how old are you?** 何歳ですか *nan sai desu ka?*; **old people** お年寄り *otoshiyori*

on に *ni*, の上に *no ue ni*; **it's on at** ... でやっている ... *de yatte iru*

once 一度 *ichi do*, 一回 *ikkai*; **once a day/an hour** 一日一回・一時間に一回 *ichi nichi ikkai/ichi jikan ni ikkai*

one 一 *ichi*

only だけ *dake*

open *(adj)* 開いている *aite iru*

open *(vt)* 開ける *akeru*; *(vi)* 開く *hiraku*

operation: to have an operation 手術を受ける *shujutsu o ukeru*

opinion 意見 *iken*; **in my opinion** 私の意見としては *watashi no iken to shite wa*

opportunity 機会 *kikai*

opposite *(n)* 反対 *hantai*

opposite *(prep)* ... の反対 ... *no hantai*

optician 眼鏡技師 *megane gishi*

or か *ka*

orange オレンジ *orenji*

orchestra オーケストラ *ôkesutora*

order *(n)* *(of food)* 注文 *chûmon*; **out of order** 故障中 *koshô chû*

order *(v)* 注文する *chûmon suru* **51, 52**

organic *(food)* 無農薬 *munôyaku*

organize 手配する *tehai suru*

other 他の *hoka no* ...; **others** それ以外のもの *sore igai no mono*

otherwise さもなければ *samo nakereba*
outside 外 *soto*
oven オーブン *ôbun*
over … の上に … *no ue ni*; **over there** あちら *achira*
overweight *(thing)* 重量オーバーの *jûryô ôba (no +n)*; *(person)* 太りすぎ *futorisugi*; **my luggage is overweight** 荷物が重すぎる *nimotsu ga omosugiru*
owe … に負っている … *ni otte iru* **55**
own *(adj)* 自分の *jibun no*; **my own car** マイカー *mai kâ*
own *(v)* 所有する *shoyû suru*, 持っている *motte iru*
owner 所有者 *shoyûsha*

P

Pacific Ocean 太平洋 *taihêyô*
pack 荷造りする *nizukuri suru*; **to pack one's suitcase** スーツケースに荷物を詰める *sûtsukêsu ni nimotsu o tsumeru*
package holiday パッケージツアー *pakêji tsuâ*
packet 小荷物 *konimotsu*
painting 絵 *e*, 絵画 *kaiga*
pair 一対 *ittsui*; **a pair of pyjamas** パジャマ *pajama*; **a pair of shorts** ショートパンツ *shôto pantsu*
palace 宮殿 *kyûden*
pan *(saucepan)* なべ *nabe*
pants パンツ *pantsu*
paper 紙 *kami*; **paper napkin** 紙ナプキン *kami napukin*; **paper tissue** ティッシュ *tisshu*
parcel 小包 *kozutsumi*
pardon? 何ですか *nan desu ka?*

parents *(one's own)* 両親 *ryôshin*; *(someone else's)* ご両親 *goryôshin*
park *(n)* 公園 *kôen*
park *(v)* 駐車する *chûsha suru*
parking space 駐車スペース *chûsha supêsu*
part 部分 *bubun*; **to be a part of** … の一部になる … *no ichi bu ni naru*
party パーティー *pâtî*
pass *(n)* *(document)* パス *pasu*; *(in mountain)* 峠 *tôge*
pass by 通り過ぎる *tôrisugiru*
passenger 乗客 *jôkyaku*
passport パスポート *pasupôto*
past *(adj)* 過ぎた *sugita*, 過去の *kako no*; **a quarter past ten** 10時15分 *jû ji jûgo fun*
path 小道 *komichi* **86**
patient *(adj)* 忍耐強い *nintaizuyoi*
patient *(n)* 患者 *kanja*
pay *(v)* 払う *harau*
pedestrian 歩行者 *hokôsha*
pedestrianized street 歩行者天国 *hokôsha tengoku*
pee おしっこをする *oshikko o suru*
peel *(v)* 皮をむく *kawa o muku*
pen ペン *pen*
pencil 鉛筆 *empitsu*
people 人々 *hitobito* **50**
per cent パーセント *pâsento*
perfect 完璧 *kampeki*
perfume 香水 *kôsui*
perhaps 多分 *tabun*
periods 生理 *sêri*, 月経 *gekkê*
person 人 *hito*
petrol ガソリン *gasorin* **34**
petrol station ガソリンスタンド *gasorin sutando*
Philippines フィリピン *firipin*
phone *(n)* 電話 *denwa*

phone (v) 電話する denwa suru

phone box 電話ボックス denwa bokkusu 113

phone call 電話 denwa; **to make a phone call** 電話する denwa suru

phonecard テレホンカード terehon kâdo 113

phone number 電話番号 denwa bangô

photo 写真 shashin; **to take a photo (of)** 写真を撮る shashin o toru; **to take someone's photo** … を写真に撮る … o shashin ni toru 101; **would you take a photo of me/us?** 写真を撮ってもらえませんか shashin o totte moraemasen ka?

picnic ピクニック pikunikku; **to have a picnic** ピクニックをする pikunikku o suru

pie パイ pai

piece ひとつ hitotsu; **a piece of** … を一切れ … o hito kire; **a piece of fruit** フルーツを一切れ furûtsu o hito kire

piles 痔 ji

pill 錠剤 jôzai; (contraceptive) ピル piru; **to be on the pill** ピルを飲んでいる piru o nonde iru 121

pillow 枕 makura

pillowcase 枕カバー makura kabâ

PIN (number) 暗証番号 anshô bangô

pink (n) ピンク pinku

pink (adj) ピンクの pinku no

pity: it's a pity 残念ですね zannen desu ne

place 場所 basho, 所 tokoro

plan 計画 kêkaku

plane 飛行機 hikôki

plant 植物 shokubutsu

plaster (cast) ギプス gipusu

plastic プラスチック purasuchikku, ビニール binîru

plastic bag ビニール袋 binîru bukuro

plate 皿 sara

platform ホーム hômu 32

play (n) 芝居 shibai, 劇 geki

play (v) (children) 遊ぶ asobu; (instrument) 弾く hiku; (sport) する suru

please お願いします onegai shimasu

pleased うれしい ureshî; **pleased to meet you!** どうぞ、よろしく dôzo yoroshiku

pleasure 喜び yorokobi

plug (electric) プラグ puragu

plug in コンセントにプラグを差し込む konsento ni puragu o sashikomu

plumber 配管工 haikankô

point (v) 点 ten

police 警察 kêsatsu

policeman 警察官 kêsatsukan

police station 警察署 kêsatsusho 125

police woman 婦人警官 fujin kêkan

poor 貧しい mazushî, 貧乏な bimbô na

port 港 minato

portrait 肖像画 shôzôga

possibility 可能性 kanôsê

possible 可能な kanô na

post (n) 郵便 yûbin

post (v) 投函する tôkan suru

postbox ポスト posuto 107

postcard はがき hagaki; **picture postcard** 絵葉書 ehagaki

postcode 郵便番号 yûbin bangô

poster ポスター *posutâ*
postman 郵便配達 *yûbin haitatsu*
post office 郵便局 *yûbinkyoku* **107**
pound ポンド *pondo*
powder 粉 *kona*; (medicine) 散剤 *sanzai*
practical 現実的な *genjitsuteki na*
pram 乳母車 *ubaguruma*, ベビーカー *bêbî kâ*
prefer 好む *konomu*
pregnant 妊娠している *ninshin shite iru* **121**
prepare 準備する *jumbi suru*
present (adj) 今の *ima no*
present (n) プレゼント *purezento* **98**
press 押さえる *osaeru*; (iron) アイロンをかける *airon o kakeru*
pressure 圧力 *atsuryoku*, プレッシャー *pureshâ*
previous 前の *mae no*
price 値段 *nedan*
private 個人的な *kojinteki na*; (organization) 私立の *shiritsu (no + n)*
prize 賞 *shô*
probably 多分 *tabun*
problem 問題 *mondai*
procession 行進 *kôshin*
product 製品 *sêhin*
profession 職業 *shokugyô*
programme (for theatre etc) プログラム *puroguramu*; (on TV) 番組 *bangumi*
promise (n) 約束 *yakusoku*
promise (v) 約束する *yakusoku suru*
propose 提案する *têan suru*; (marriage) プロポーズする *puropôzu suru*
protect 守る *mamoru*
proud 誇りに思う *hokori ni omô*

public 公的な *kôteki na*; (organization) 公立の *kôritsu (no + n)*
public holiday 祝日 *shukujitsu*
pull 引く *hiku*
purple (n) 紫色 *murasaki iro*
purple (adj) 紫の *murasaki no*
purpose 目的 *mokuteki*; **on purpose** わざと *waza to*
purse 財布 *saifu*
push 押す *osu*
pushchair 乳母車 *ubaguruma*, ベビーカー *bêbî kâ*
put 置く *oku*
put out (extinguish) 消す *kesu*
put up with 我慢する *gaman suru*

Q

quality 質 *shitsu*; **of good/bad quality** 質がいい・悪い *shitsu ga î/warui*
quarter 四分の一 *yom bun no ichi*; **a quarter of an hour** 十五分 *jûgo fun*; **a quarter to ten** 十時十五分前 *jû ji jûgo fun mae*
quay 波止場 *hatoba*
question 質問 *shitsumon*
queue (n) 行列 *gyôretsu*
queue (v) 列を作る *retsu o tsukuru*
quick 速い *hayai*
quickly 速く *hayaku*
quiet 静かな *shizuka na*
quite かなり *kanari*; **quite a lot of** かなりたくさん *kanari takusan*

R

racist 人種差別主義者 *jinshu sabetsu shugi sha*

racket ラケット *raketto*

radiator *(on car)* ラジエーター *rajiêtâ*

radio ラジオ *rajio*

rare 珍しい *mezurashî; (meat)* レア *rea*

rarely めったにない *metta ni nai*

rather *(quite)* かなり *kanari*

raw 生の *nama (no + n)*

razor かみそり *kamisori*

razor blade かみそりの刃 *kamisori no ha*

reach 届く *todoku*

read 読む *yomu*

ready 用意のできた *yôi no dekita*

reasonable *(person, behaviour)* 分別のある *fumbetsu no aru; (price)* まあまあ *mâmâ*

receipt レシート *reshîto*, 領収書 *ryôshûsho* 121

receive 受け取る *uketoru*

reception *(in hotel)* フロント *furonto; at reception* フロントで *furonto de*

receptionist 受付係 *uketsuke gakari*

recipe 調理法 *chôrihô*, レシピ *reshipi*

recognize 認める *mitomeru*

recommend 薦める *susumeru* 41, 48, 86

red *(n)* 赤 *aka*

red *(adj)* 赤い *akai; red hair* 赤毛 *akage*

red light 赤信号 *aka shingô*

reduce 減少させる *genshô saseru*

reduction *(in price)* 値下げ *nesage*

red wine 赤ワイン *aka wain*

refrigerator 冷蔵庫 *rêzôko*

refund *(n)* 払い戻し *haraimodoshi*, 返金 *henkin; to get a refund* 払

い戻してもらう *haraimodoshite morau*

refund *(v)* 払い戻す *haraimodosu*

refuse *(v)* 断る *kotowaru*

registration number 登録番号 *tôroku bangô; (for car)* プレートナンバー *purêto nambâ*

remember 思い出す *omoidasu*

remind 思い出させる *omoidasaseru*

remove 取り去る *torisaru*

rent *(n)* 家賃 *yachin*, レンタルする *rentaru suru*

rent *(v)* 賃借りする *chingari suru* 45

rent-a-car レンタカー *rentakâ*

rental レンタル *rentaru*

reopen 再開する *saikai suru*

repair *(v)* 修理する *shûri suru* 35; **to get something repaired** 修理してもらう *shûri shite morau*

repeat 繰り返す *kurikaesu*

reserve *(v)* 予約する *yoyaku suru* 41, 49, 50

reserved 予約してある *yoyaku shite aru; (seat)* 予約席 *yoyaku seki*

rest *(n) (repose)* 休憩 *kyûkê; the rest (remainder)* 残り *nokori*

rest *(v)* 休む *yasumu*, 休憩する *kyûkê suru*

restaurant レストラン *resutoran* 48

return *(v)* 戻る *modoru*

return ticket 往復(切符) *ôfuku (kippu)*

reverse-charge call コレクトコール *korekuto kôru* 113

reverse gear バックギア *bakku gia*

rheumatism リューマチ *ryûmachi*

rib あばら肉 *abara niku*, リブ *ribu*

right (n) (direction) 右 migi; (legal) 権利 kenri; **to have the right to … する権利がある** … suru kenri ga aru; **to the right of** … の右 … no migi

right (adj) 正しい tadashî

right (adv) (correctly) 正しく tadashiku; **right away** すぐに sugu ni; **right beside** すぐ隣に sugu tonari ni

ring 輪 wa; (jewellery) 指輪 yubiwa

ripe 熟した juku shita

rip-off ぼったくり bottakuri

risk 危険性 kikensê

river 川 kawa

road 道路 dôro

road sign 交通標識 kôtsû hyôshiki

rock 岩 iwa

rollerblades ローラーブレード rôrâburêdo

room 部屋 heya **41, 42**

rosé wine ロゼワイン roze wain

round (adj) 丸い marui; **to go round** (garden etc) 回って行く mawatte iku

rubbish ごみ gomi; **to take the rubbish out** ごみを出す gomi o dasu

rucksack リュックサック ryukkusakku

ruins 廃墟 haikyo; **in ruins** 廃墟 になった haikyo ni natta

run 走る hashiru

run out なくなる naku naru; **to have run out of petrol** ガソリ ンが切れた gasorin ga kireta

S

sad 悲しい kanashî

safe (adj) 安全な anzen na

safe (n) 金庫 kinko

safety 安全 anzen

safety belt シートベルト shîto beruto

sail 帆走する hansô suru

sailing: to go sailing ヨットを走 らせる yotto o hashiraseru

sale: for sale セール sêru; **in the sale** セールで sêru de; **on sale** 販 売中 hambai chû

salt 塩 shio

salted 塩で味付けされた shio de aji tsukesareta

salty 塩辛い shiokarai

same 同じ onaji; **the same** 同一 の dôitsu (no + n) **54**

sand 砂 suna

sandals サンダル sandaru

sanitary towel 生理用ナプキン sêri yô napukin

Saturday 土曜日 doyôbi

save (rescue) 救う sukû; (money) 貯 金する chokin suru

say 言う yû; **how do you say …?** 何と言いますか … nan to îmasu ka …?

scared: to be scared of 怖い kowai

scenery 景色 keshiki

scissors はさみ hasami

scooter スクーター sukûtâ

scotch (whisky) スコッチ sukotchi

Scotland スコットランド sukottorando

Scottish (adj) スコットラン ドの sukottorando no; **Scottish person** スコットランド人 sukottorandojin

scuba diving スキューバダイビ ング sukyûbâ daibingu

sea 海 umi

seafood シーフード shîfûdo

seasick 船酔い *funayoi*; **to be seasick** 船に酔う *fune ni you*

seaside: at the seaside 海辺で *umibe de*

season 季節 *kisetsu*

seat 席 *seki* **27**

seaweed 海草 *kaisô*

second 二番目 *nibamme*

secondary school (12–15 years old) 中学校 *chûgakkô*; (15–18 years old) 高校 *kôkô*

second-hand 中古の *chûko (no + n)*

secure 安全な *anzen na*, 確実な *kakujitsu na*

security 安全 *anzen*; (protection) 警備 *kêbi*

see 見る *miru*; **see you later!** じゃ、また後で *ja, mata ato de*; **see you soon!** じゃ、また *ja, mata*; **see you tomorrow!** じゃ、また明日 *ja, mata ashita*

seem 見える *mieru*; **it seems that** … のように見える … *no yô ni mieru*

seldom めったにない *metta ni nai*

self-confidence 自信 *jishin*

sell 売る *uru*

Sellotape® セロテープ *serotêpu*

send 送る *okuru*

sender (of parcel) 送り主 *okurinushi*; (of letter) 差出人 *sashidashinin*

sense 感覚 *kankaku*

sentence 文章 *bunsho*

separate (vi) 別れる *wakareru*; (vt) 分ける *wakeru*

separately 別々に *betsubetsu ni* **55**

September 九月 *kugatsu*

serious (person) まじめな *majime na*; (situation) 深刻な *shinkoku na*

several いくつかの *ikutsuka (no + n)*

sex (gender) 性 *sê*; (intercourse) セックス *sekkusu*

shade かげ *kage*; (colour) 色合い *iroai*; **in the shade** 陰に *kage ni*

shame 恥 *haji*; **it's a shame** 残念ですね *zannen desu ne*

shampoo シャンプー *shampû*

shape 形 *katachi*

share (v) 分ける *wakerue*

shave そる *soru*

shaving cream シェービングクリーム *shêbingu kurîmu*

shaving foam シェービングフォーム *shêbingu fômu*

she 彼女 *kanojo*

sheet シーツ *shîtsu*

shellfish 貝 *kai*

shirt シャツ *shatsu*

shock ショック *shokku*

shocking ショッキングな *shokkingu na*

shoes 靴 *kutsu*

shop 店 *mise*

shop assistant 店員 *ten'in*

shopkeeper 店員 *ten'in*

shopping 買い物 *kaimono*; **to do some/the shopping** 買い物をする *kaimono o suru*

shopping centre ショッピングセンター *shoppingu sentâ*, モール *môru*

short 短い *mijikai*

short cut 近道 *chika michi*

shorts ショートパンツ *shôto pantsu*

short-sleeved 半袖 *han sode*

shoulder 肩 *kata*

show (n) ショー *shô* **74**

show (v) 見せる *miseru*

shower シャワー *shawâ*; **to take a shower** シャワーを浴びる *shawâ o abiru*

shower gel シャワージェル *shawâ jeru*

shrine 神社 *jinja*

shut (v) 閉じる *tôjiru*

shuttle bus シャトルバス *shattoru basu*

shy 恥ずかしがりの *hazukashigari (no + n)*

sick 病気 *byôki*; **to feel sick** 吐き気がする *hakike ga suru*

side 横 *yoko*; **right-hand side** (右)側 *(migi) gawa*; **left-hand side** (左)側 *(hidari) gawa*

sign (n) (on shop, building) 看板 *kamban*; (on road) 標識 *hyôshiki*

sign (v) サインする *sain suru*, 署名する *shomê suru*

signal 信号 *shingô*

signature サイン *sain*, 署名 *shomê*

silent 音がしない *oto ga shinai*

silk 絹 *kinu*

silver 銀 *gin*

since … から … *kara*

sing 歌う *utau*

singer 歌手 *kashu*

single (one only) ひとつの *hitotsu (no + n)*; (unmarried) 独身 *dokushin*

single (ticket) 片道切符 *katamichi (kippu)*

sister (elder – one's own) 姉 *ane*; (– someone else's) お姉さん *onê-san*; (younger – one's own) 妹 *imôto*; (– someone else's) 妹さん *imôto-san*

sit down 座る *suwaru*

size サイズ *saizu* **97**

ski (n) スキー *sukî*

ski (v) スキーをする *sukî o suru*

ski boots スキー靴 *sukî gutsu*

skiing スキー *sukî*; **to go skiing** スキーに行く *sukî ni iku*

ski lift リフト *rifuto*

skin 肌 *hada*

ski pole スキーストック *sukî sutokku*

ski resort スキー場 *sukî jô*

skirt スカート *sukâto*

sky 空 *sora*

skyscraper 超高層ビル *chôkôsô biru*

sleep (n) 睡眠 *suimin*

sleep (v) 寝る *neru*; **to sleep with** … と寝る … *to neru*

sleeping bag 寝袋 *nebukuro*

sleeping pill 睡眠薬 *suimin yaku*

sleepy: to be sleepy 眠い *nemui*

sleeve 袖 *sode*

slice (n) 薄切り *usugiri*

slice (v) 薄く切る *usuku kiru*

sliced 薄切りにした *usugiri ni shita*

slide スライド *suraido*

slow 遅い *osoi*; (positive meaning) ゆっくりした *yukkuri shita*

slowly ゆっくりと *yukkuri to*

small 小さい *chîsai*

smell (n) におい *nioi*

smell (v) におう *niou*; **to smell good/bad** いいにおい・変なにおいがする *î nioi/hen na nioi ga suru*

smile (n) ほほえみ *hohoemi*

smile (v) ほほえむ *hohoemu*, 笑う *warau*

smoke (n) 煙 *kemuri*

smoke (v) タバコを吸う *tabako o sû*

smoker 喫煙者 *kitsuensha*

snack 軽食 *kêshoku*, おやつ *oyatsu*

snow (n) 雪 *yuki*

snow (v) 雪が降る *yuki ga furu*

so: so that だから *dakara*

soap せっけん *sekken*

soccer サッカー *sakkâ*

socks ソックス *sokkusu*, 靴下 *kutsushita*

some いくらかの *ikura ka (no + n)*; **some people** ある人たち *aru hitotachi*

somebody, someone 誰か *dare ka*

something 何か *nani ka*; **something else** 他のもの *hoka no mono*

sometimes ときどき *tokidoki*

somewhere どこか *doko ka*; **somewhere else** どこか他の所 *doko ka hoka no tokoro*

son (one's own) 息子 *musuko*; (someone else's) 息子さん *musuko-san*

song 歌 *uta*

soon もうすぐ *môsugu*

spice スパイス *supaisu*

spicy 辛い *karai*

spider クモ *kumo*

splinter とげ *toge*

spoil (food) だめになる *dame ni naru*

sponge スポンジ *suponji*

spoon スプーン *supûn*

sport スポーツ *supôtsu*

sports ground 競技場 *kyôgijô*

sporty 運動神経のいい *undô shinkê no î*

spot (place) 場所 *basho*; (on skin) 吹き出物 *fukidemono*

sprain くじく *kujiku*, 捻挫する *nenza suru*; **to sprain one's ankle** 足首を捻挫する *ashikubi o nenza suru*

spring (season) 春 *haru*; (water) 泉 *izumi*; (wire) ばね *bane*

stadium スタジアム *stajiamu*

stain (n) しみ *shimi*

stairs 階段 *kaidan*

stamp 切手 *kitte* **107**

start (vt) 始める *hajimeru*; (vi) 始まる *hajimaru*

state (condition) 状態 *jôtai*

statement 声明 *sêmê*

station 駅 *eki*

stay (n) 滞在 *taizai*

stay (v) 滞在する *taizai suru*; **to stay in touch** 連絡を保つ *renraku o tamotsu*

steal 盗む *nusumu*

steering wheel ハンドル *handoru*

step (stair) 段 *dan*

sticking plaster 絆創膏 *bansôkô*

still (adv) まだ *mada*

still (adj) 動かない *ugokanai*

sting (n) 針 *hari*

sting (v) 刺す *sasu*; **to get stung (by)** … に刺される *… ni sasareru*

stock: out of stock 在庫切れ *zaiko gire*

stomach おなか *onaka*

stone 石 *ishi*

stop (n) 停止 *têshi*

stop (v) 止まる *tomaru*

stopcock 栓 *sen*

storey 階 *kai*

storm 嵐 *arashi*

straight ahead, straight on まっすぐ *massugu*

strange 変な *hen na*, おかしい *okashî*

street 通り *tôri*

strong 強い *tsuyoi*; (tea) 濃い *koi*

stuck 動かない *ugokanai*

student 学生 *gakusê* **26**

studies 勉強 *benkyô*

study (v) 勉強する *benkyô suru*; **to study biology** 生物学を勉強する *sêbutsugaku o benkyô suru*

style スタイル *sutairu*

subtitled 字幕つきの *jimaku tsuki (no + n)*

suburb 郊外 *kôgai*

suffer 苦しむ *kurushimu*

sugar 砂糖 *satô*

suggest 提案する *têan suru*

suit (n) スーツ *sûtsu*

suit (v) 合う *au*; **does that suit you?** それでいいですか *sore de î desu ka?*

suitcase スーツケース *sûtsukêsu* **28**

summer 夏 *natsu*

summit 頂上 *chôjô*

sun 太陽 *taiyô*, 日 *hi*; **in the sun** 日のもとで *hi no moto de*

sunbathe 日光浴する *nikkôyoku suru*

sun block 日焼け止めクリーム *hiyakedome kurîmu*

sunburnt: to get sunburnt 日焼けする *hiyake suru*

Sunday 日曜日 *nichiyôbi*

sunglasses サングラス *sangurasu*

sunhat 日よけ帽 *hiyori bô*

sunrise 日の出 *hi no de*

sunset 日の入り *hi no iri*

sunstroke 日射病 *nisshabyô*; **to get sunstroke** 日射病にかかる *nisshabyô ni kakaru*

supermarket スーパー *sûpâ* **45, 91**

supplement (extra charge) 追加料金 *tsuika ryôkin*

sure: to be sure 確信している *kakushin shite iru*

surgical spirit 消毒用アルコール *shôdoku yô arukôru*

surname 苗字 *myôji*, 姓 *myôji/sê*

surprised: to be surprised 驚く *odoroku*, びっくりする *bikkuri suru*

sweat (n) 汗 *ase*

sweat (v) 汗をかく *ase o kaku*

sweater セーター *sêtâ*

sweatshirt トレーナー *torênâ*

sweet (n) 菓子 *kashi*

sweet (adj) 甘い *amai*

swim (n) **to go for a swim** 泳ぎに行く *oyogi ni iku*

swim (v) 泳ぐ *oyogu*

swimming 水泳 *suiê*

swimming pool プール *pûru*

swimming trunks 水泳パンツ *suiê pantsu*

swimsuit 水着 *mizugi*

switch off スイッチを切る *suitchi o kiru*; (light) 消す *kesu*

switch on スイッチを入れる *suitchi o ireru*; (light) つける *tsukeru*

switchboard operator 電話交換手 *denwa kôkanshu*

swollen はれた *hareta*, ふくれた *fukureta*

synagogue シナゴーグ *shinagôgu*

T

table テーブル *têburu* **49, 50**

tablespoon 大さじ *ôsaji*

tablet 錠剤 *jôzai*

Taiwan 台湾 *taiwan*

take 取る *toru*; (time) かかる *kakaru*; **it takes two hours** 二時間かかる *ni jikan kakaru*

takeaway お持ち帰り *omochikaeri*

take off (plane) 離陸する *ririku suru*

talk 話す *hanasu*

tall (person) 背が高い *se ga takai*

tampon タンポン *tampon*

tap 蛇口 *jaguchi*

taste (n) (flavour) 味 *aji*; (preference) 好み *konomi*

taste (v) 味見をする *ajimi o suru*

tax 税金 *zêkin*

tax-free 免税 *menzê*

taxi タクシー *takushî* **35**

taxi driver タクシーの運転手 *takushî no untenshu*

tea (Japanese) お茶 *ocha*; (black) 紅茶 *kôcha*

team チーム *chîmu*

teaspoon 小さじ *kosaji*

teenager ティーンエージャー *tîn'êjâ*

telephone (n) 電話 *denwa*

telephone (v) 電話する *denwa suru*

television テレビ *terebi*

tell 言う *yû*

temperature (of weather) 温度 *ondo*; **to take one's temperature** 体温を測る *taion o hakaru*

temple (お) 寺 *(o)tera*

temporary 臨時の *rinji no*, 一時的な *ichijiteki na*

tennis テニス *tenisu*

tennis court テニスコート *tenisu kôto*

tennis shoe テニスシューズ *tenisu shûzu*

tent テント *tento*

tent peg テントのくい *tento no kui*

terminal (n) ターミナル *tâminaru*, 終点 *shûten*

terrace テラス *terasu*

terrible ひどい *hidoi*

Thailand タイ *tai*

thank (v) 感謝する *kansha suru*; **thank you** ありがとうございます *arigatô gozaimasu*; **thank you very much** どうもありがとうございます *dômo arigatô gozaimasu*

thanks ありがとう *arigatô*; **thanks to** … のおかげで … *no okage de*

that あの *ano + n*; **that one** あれ *are*

theatre 劇場 *gekijo*

theft 盗み *nusumi*

theme park テーマパーク *têma pâku*

then それから *sore kara*

there そこ *soko*; **there is/there are** (people, animals) … がいる … *ga iru*; (things) … がある … *ga aru*

therefore だから *dakara*

thermometer 温度計 *ondôkê*

these この *kono + n*; **these ones** これ *kore*

they (people) 彼ら *kare ra*; (others) それ *sore*

thief 泥棒 *dorobô*

thigh もも *momo*

thin 細い *hosoi*

thing もの *mono*

think 考える *kangaeru*, 思う *omô*

think about … について考える … *ni tsuite kangaeru*

thirsty: to be thirsty のどが渇いた *nodo ga kawaita*

this この *kono + n*; **this one** これ *kore*; **this evening** 今晩 *komban*; **this is** これは … だ *kore wa … da*

those その *sono + n*, あの *ano + n*; **those ones** それ *sore*, あれ *are*

throat のど *nodo*

throw 投げる *nageru*

throw out 捨てる *suteru*

Thursday 木曜日 *mokuyôbi*

ticket チケット *chiketto*, 切符 *kippu* **26**, **73**, **74**, **80**

ticket office チケット *chiketto*, 切符売り場 *kippu uriba*

tidy きちんとした *kichin to shita*

tie (n) ネクタイ *nekutai*

tie (v) 結ぶ *musubu*

tight きつい *kitsui*

tights パンスト *pansuto*

time 時間 *jikan* **136**; **what time is it?** 何時ですか *nan ji desu ka?*; **from time to time** ときどき *tokidoki*; **on time** 時間通り *jikan dôri*; **three/four times** 三・四回 *san kai/yon kai*

time difference 時差 *jisa*

timetable 時刻表 *jikokuhyô* **26**

tinfoil アルミ箔 *arumihaku*

tired 疲れた *tsukareta*

tobacco タバコ *tabako*

tobacconist's タバコ屋 *tabako ya*

today 今日 *kyô*

together 一緒に *issho ni*

toilet トイレ *toire*, お手洗い *otearai* **49**

toilet bag 化粧ポーチ *keshô pôchi*

toilet paper トイレットペーパー *toiretto pêpâ*

toiletries 化粧品 *keshôhin*

toll 通行料 *tsûkôryô*

tomorrow 明日 *ashita*; **tomorrow evening** 明日の晩 *ashita no ban*; **tomorrow morning** 明日の朝 *ashita no asa*

tongue 舌 *shita*

tonight 今夜 *kon'ya*, 今晩 *komban*

too (+ adj) …すぎる (adj without final i for "i" adjectives – see grammar chapter) + sugiru; (as well – only after n) …も… *mo*; **too big** 大きすぎる *ôkisugiru*; **too quiet** 静かすぎる *shizukasugiru*; **me too** 私も *watashi mo*; **too many** 多すぎる *ôsugiru*

tooth 歯 *ha*

toothbrush 歯ブラシ *haburashi*

toothpaste 歯磨き *hamigaki*

top 上 *ue*; **at the top** 一番上で *ichi ban ue de*

torch 懐中電灯 *kaichû dentô*

touch 触れる *fureru*

tourist 観光客 *kankô kyaku*

tourist office 観光案内所 *kankô annaijo* **78**

tourist trap 観光名所 *kankô mêsho*

towards …の方へ *… no hô e*

towel タオル *taoru*

town 町 *machi*

town centre 中心街 *chûshingai*

town hall 市役所 *shiyakusho*

toy おもちゃ *omocha*

traditional 伝統的な *dentôteki na*

traffic 交通 *kôtsû*

traffic jam 交通渋滞 *kôtsû jûtai*

train 列車 *ressha* **31**, **32**; **the train to Kyoto** 京都行きの列車 *kyôto yuki no ressha*

trainers 運動靴 *undô gutsu*

train station 駅 *eki*

tram 路面電車 *romen densha*, 市電 *shiden*

transfer (v) (money) 振り込む *furikomu* **105**

translate 翻訳する *hon'yaku suru*

travel 旅行 *ryokô*

travel agency 旅行代理店 *ryokô dairiten*

traveller's cheque トラベラーズチェック *toraberâzu chekku*

tree 木 *ki*

trip 旅 *tabi*; **have a good trip!** よい旅行を *yoi ryokô o!*

trolley カート *kâto*

trouble 問題 *mondai*

trousers ズボン *zubon*

true 本当の *hontô (no + n)*

try 試みる *kokoromiru*; **to try to do something** やってみる *yatte miru*

try on 着てみる *kite miru* **96**

Tuesday 火曜日 *kayôbi*

tube (underground) 地下鉄 chikatetsu

tube station 地下鉄の駅 chikatetsu no eki

turn (n) 順番 junban; **it's your turn** あなたの番だ anata no ban da

turn (v) (round) 回転する kaiten suru; (at corner) 曲がる magaru

twice 二度 ni do, 二回 ni kai

type (n) タイプ taipu, 種類 shurui

type (v) タイプを打つ taipu o utsu

typhoon 台風 taifû

typical 典型的な tenkêteki na

tyre タイヤ taiya

U

umbrella 傘 kasa

uncle (one's own) おじ oji; (someone else's) おじさん oji-san

uncomfortable 居心地が悪い igokochi ga warui

under (location) … の下に … no shita; (less than) 以下 ika

underground 地下鉄 chikatetsu 31

underground line 地下鉄線 chikatetsu sen

underground station 地下鉄の駅 chikatetsu no eki

underneath … の下に … no shita ni

understand 分かる wakaru 12

underwear 下着 shitagi

United Kingdom 英国 êkoku, イギリス igirisu

United States アメリカ amerika, 米国 bêkoku

until … まで … made

upset: to get upset うろたえる urotaeru; **to have an upset stomach** 気持ちが悪くなった kimochi ga waruku natta; **don't get upset** 落ち着きなさい ochitsukinasai

upstairs 階上 kaijô

urgent 緊急 kinkyû

use (v) 使う tsukau; **to be used for** … に使う … ni tsukau; **I'm used to it** 慣れている narete iru

useful 役に立つ yaku ni tatsu

useless むだな muda na

usually 普通 futsû

U-turn Uターン yûtân

V

vaccinated (against) (… の) 予防接種を受けた (… no) yobô sesshu o uketa

valid (for) 有効な yûkô na **80**

valley 谷 tani

vegetarian 菜食主義者 saishoku shugi sha

very とても totemo

video camera ビデオカメラ bideo kamera

view (scenery) 眺め nagame, 見晴らし miharashi; (opinion) 見方 mikata

village 村 mura

visa ビザ biza

visit (n) 訪問 hômon

visit (v) 訪ねる tazuneru, 訪問する hômon suru

volleyball バレー barê

vomit (v) 吐く haku

W

waist ウエスト uesuto

wait 待つ matsu; **to wait for** … を待つ … o matsu

waiter ウエイター *ueitâ*
waitress ウエイトレス *ueitoresu*
wake up 目が覚める *me ga sameru*
Wales ウェールズ *wêruzu*
walk (n) 散歩 *sampo* **86**; **to go for a walk** 散歩する *sampo suru*
walk (v) 歩く *aruku*
walking boots ウォーキングブーツ *wôkingu bûtsu*
wallet 財布 *saifu*
want ほしい *hoshî* (see grammar)
warm 暖かい *atatakai*
warn 注意する *chûi suru*
wash (v) 洗う *arau*; **to wash one's hair** 髪を洗う *kami o arau*
washbasin 洗面台 *semmendai*
washing 洗濯 *sentaku*; **to do the washing** 洗濯する *sentaku suru*
washing machine 洗濯機 *sentakki*
washing powder 洗剤 *senzai*
washing-up liquid 食器用洗剤 *shokki yô senzai*
wasp スズメバチ *suzumebachi*
waste (n) 浪費 *rôhi*
waste (v) むだにする *muda ni suru*
watch (n) 腕時計 *ude dokê*
watch (v) 見る *miru*; **watch out!** 危ない *abunai!*
water (cold) 水 *mizu*; (hot) お湯 *oyu* **52**
waterproof 防水 *bôsui*
waterskiing ウォータースキー *wôtâsukî*
wave 波 *nami*
way (route) 道 *michi*; (method) 方法 *hôhô*
way in 入口 *iriguchi*
way out 出口 *deguchi*
we 私たち *watashi-tachi*
weak 弱い *yowai*
wear 着る *kiru*; (on legs/feet) はく *haku*; (on head) かぶる *kaburu*
weather 天気 *tenki*; **the weather's bad** 天気が悪い *tenki ga warui*
weather forecast 天気予報 *tenki yohô* **23**
website ウェブサイト *webusaito*
Wednesday 水曜日 *suiyôbi*
week 週 *shû*; (period) 週間 *shûkan*
weekend 週末 *shûmatsu*
welcome 歓迎する *kangê suru*; **welcome!** ようこそ *yôkoso*; **you're welcome** どういたしまして *dô itashimashite*
well: I'm very well 元気です *genki desu*; **well done** (meat) ウェルダン *werudan*
well-known 有名な *yûmê na*
Welsh (n) (language) ウェールズ語 *wêruzugo*
Welsh (adj) ウェールズの *wêruzu no*; **Welsh person** ウェールズ人 *wêruzujin*
west 西 *nishi*; **in the west** 西に *nishi ni*; **(to the) west of …** … の西 … *no nishi*
wet 濡れた *nureta*
wetsuit ウェットスーツ *uettosûtsu*
what なに *nani*, なん *nan*; **what do you want?** 何がほしいですか *nani ga hoshî desu ka?*
wheel 車輪 *sharin*
wheelchair 車椅子 *kuruma isu*
when いつ *itsu*
where どこ *doko*; **where is/are …?** …どこですか … *doko desu ka?*; **where are you from?** どこから来ましたか *doko kara kimashita ka?*; **where are you going?** どこへ行きますか *doko e ikimasu ka?*

which どの (+ n) dono; (which one) どれ dore

white (n) 白 shiro

white (adj) 白い shiroi

white wine 白ワイン shiro wain

who 誰 dare; (more polite) どなた donata; **who's calling?** どちら様ですか dochira sama desu ka?

whole 全体 zentai; **the whole cake** ケーキ全部 kêki zembu

whose 誰の dare no ...

why なぜ naze, どうして dôshite

wide 広い hiroi

wife (one's own) 妻 tsuma, 家内 kanai; (someone else's) 奥さん oku-san

wild (animal, flower) 野生の yasê (no + n)

wind 風 kaze

window 窓 mado; **in the window** 窓に mado ni

windscreen フロントガラス furonto garasu

windsurfing ウインドサーフィン uindosâfin

wine ワイン wain **52, 53**

winter 冬 fuyu

with ... と一緒に ... to issho ni

withdraw (money) (お金を) 引き出す (okane o) hikidasu

without ... なしで ... nashi de

woman 女性 josê, 女の人 onna no hito

wonderful すばらしい subarashî

wood (material) 木材 mokuzai; (trees) 林 hayashi

wool ウール ûru

work (n) 仕事 shigoto; **work of art** 芸術作品 gêjutsu sakuhin

work (v) 働く hataraku

world 世界 sekai

worse もっと悪い motto warui; **to get worse** 悪くなる waruku naru; **it's worse (than)** ... より悪い ... yori warui

worth (n) 価値 kachi; **it's worth it** 価値がある kachi ga aru

wound 傷 kizu, けが kega

wrist 手首 tekubi

write 書く kaku **12**

wrong 間違っている machigatte iru

XYZ

X-rays レントゲン rentogen

year 年 toshi/nen

yellow (n) 黄色 kîro

yellow (adj) 黄色い kîroi

yes はい hai; (informal) ええ ê

yesterday 昨日 kinô; **yesterday evening** タベ yûbe

you あなた anata (use person's name instead if possible)

young 若い wakai

youth hostel ユースホステル yûsu hosuteru

zero ゼロ zero

zip ファスナー fasunâ, チャック chakku

zoo 動物園 dôbutsuen

zoom (lens) ズーム zûmu

GRAMMAR

Introduction

Japanese grammar works very differently from English in many ways:

- The word order in a sentence is different from English. Most importantly, verbs come at the end of the sentence. For example, the sentence "I eat sushi" becomes "I sushi eat" (*watashi wa sushi o tabemasu*). This means you have to wait until the end of the sentence to know what the verb is and whether it is affirmative or negative, present or past, a statement or a question, and so on.

- There is no difference between singular and plural; for example, *hon* can mean "book" or "books"; the context usually makes it clear which is meant. There are also various suffixes (word endings) that can be added for clarification if necessary, particularly when referring to people: *watashi* I, *watashi-tachi* we.

- There are no definite and indefinite articles ("the" or "a/some").

- Verbs have two tenses: present/future and past.

- Verbs do not change their form according to grammatical person (I, you, he, she, we, they). They do, however, change their form according to level of politeness and formality. In this phrasebook, the polite level is used for almost all phrases that you will use, and the very polite level is used for phrases you might hear from shop assistants, hotel staff, etc.

- Personal pronouns (I, he, she, it, you, we, they) are not used much; their overuse can seem rude or aggressive. The sentence *ocha o nomimasu* could therefore mean "I/you/he/she/we/they drink(s) tea". Context makes it clear who is being referred to, and the different levels of politeness also help to do this.

- Small words called particles are used to show the grammatical relationships between different parts of the sentence. These will be explained in more detail below.

- There are two kinds of adjectives, one of which has different forms as verbs do to show tense (present or past), affirmative or negative ("new" or "not new") and level of politeness and formality. They all come before the noun they describe, as in English: *atarashî hon* "new book".

- There are no relative clauses; instead, the descriptive phrase is placed before the noun, For example, "the book **that I bought yesterday** is very interesting" becomes "the **I-bought-yesterday** book is very interesting" *kinô katta hon wa totemo omoshiroi desu*.

Verbs

Japanese distinguishes between two different meanings covered by the English verb "to be": 1) existence and 2) equivalence (describing something in some way). It also uses different verbs to refer to the existence of animate and inanimate objects. So, "there is someone over there" (ie "someone exists over there") is *asoko ni hito ga imasu*, and "there is a book over there" is *asoko ni hon ga arimasu*. To describe something or someone in some way, a special verb is used, called the copula: *da* in the plain form or *desu* in the polite form. Here are two examples:

> I am Japanese *watashi wa nihonjin desu*
> it's the post office *yûbinkyoku desu*

The copula works rather differently from all other verbs.

	Affirmative		Negative	
	Plain	Polite	Plain	Polite
Present/ future	*da*	*desu*	*ja arimasen*	*ja nai*
Past	*datta*	*deshita*	*ja arimasen deshita*	*ja nakatta*

NB *ja* is a contraction of the more formal *de wa*.

All other verbs are divided into three groups, depending on their ending in the plain form.

Plain form

The plain form is used to family members and close friends. It is also used in more complex structures.

		Affirmative	Negative
Present/ future	Group 1	Plain form ends in *u*, *ku*, *gu*, *su*, *tsu*, *nu*, *bu*, *mu*, *ru*: *kau* buy, *kaku* write, *oyogu* swim, *kasu* lend, *matsu* wait, *shinu* die, *asobu* play, *nomu* drink, *noru* get on/board	"do/does not …" Change *u* ending to *anai*. Note that *au* verb endings change to *awanai* and *tsu* endings change to *tanai*: *kawanai*, *kakanai*, *oyoganai*, *kasanai*, *matanai*, *shinanai*, *asobanai*, *nomanai*, *noranai*
	Group 2	Almost all verbs ending in *eru* or *iru* (one exception is *kaeru* return, which is a Group 1 verb): *taberu* eat, *miru* see	Change *ru* ending to *nai*: *tabenai*, *minai*
	Group 3	Irregular: there are only two of these: *suru* do, *kuru* come	*shinai*, *konai*
Past	Group 1	Change *u*, *tsu*, *ru* endings to *tta*: *katta*, *matta*, *notta*. Change *ku* endings to *ita*: *kaita* NB *iku* (go) is irregular: *itta* Change *gu* endings to *ida*: *oyoida*	Change *anai* ending to *anakatta*: *kawanakatta*, *kakanakatta*, *oyoganakatta*, *kasanakatta*, *matanakatta*, *shinanakatta*, *asobanakatta*, *nomanakatta*, *noranakatta*

		Change *su* endings to *shita*: *kashita* Change *nu*, *bu*, *mu* endings to *nda*: *shinda*, *nonda*, *yonda*	
	Group 2	Change *ru* ending to *ta*: *tabeta*, *mita*	Change *nai* ending to *nakatta*: *tabenakatta*, *minakatta*
	Group 3	*shita*, *kita*	Change *nai* ending to *nakatta*: *shinakatta*, *konakatta*

Various verb stems are used as the basis of other structures. This one is probably the most useful:

Group 1	Change final *u* into *i*: *kaku* → *kaki*; *kau* → *kai* etc. NB *tsu* changes to *chi* and *su* to *shi*: *matsu* → *machi*, *kasu* → *kashi*
Group 2	Remove final *ru*: *taberu* → *tabe*
Group 3	*suru* → *shi*; *kuru* → *ki*

Polite form
Polite endings are added to this verb stem:

	Affirmative	Negative
Present/future	stem + *masu*	stem + *masen*
Past	stem + *mashita*	stem + *masen deshita*

Note that the *u* in the *-masu* ending is usually not pronounced.

Connective *-te* form
The verb form ending in *-te* is a connective form, used to link verbs to other words or phrases. It is very similar to the plain past affirmative form: simply change the final *a* to e: *katte*, *kaite*, *yonde*, etc. The *-te* form has many uses, such as joining clauses together to form longer sentences; making requests;

asking permission; expressing an ongoing or repeated action or a state. Adjectives also have -te forms used to connect them to other words and phrases. For nouns, the -te form of *desu* (de) acts in the same way.

- Longer sentences use the -te form to join clauses together. It can indicate two actions occurring at the same time, or a sequence of actions, or one action/event leading to another

    kyôto ni itte, otera to jinja o takusan mimashita I went to Kyoto and saw lots of temples and shrines
    tabesugite onaka ga itai desu I have eaten too much and (so) I have stomach ache

- The easiest way to make a request is to use the affirmative or negative -te form followed by *kudasai*

    pasupôto o misete kudasai please show me your passport
    okurenaide kudasai please don't be late

- To ask permission, add *mo î desu ka* after the -te form

    shashin o totte mo î desu ka? may I take a photo?

- Use the verb *iru (imasu)* after the -te form to describe an ongoing or repeated action, or a state. Sometimes this is equivalent to the "-ing" form in English, but not always

    shimbun o yonde imasu I'm reading a newspaper
    mai nichi densha de kaisha ni kayotte imasu I commute by train to work every day
    hiroshima ni sunde imasu I live in Hiroshima
    kuruma o motte imasu I have a car

Invitations
Negative verb forms are often used in invitations

    issho ni kimasen ka? would you like to come with me?

Another form is also used: change the *masu* ending to *mashô*

    ikimashô let's go

Add *ka* to make it into a suggestion

> *ikimashô ka?* shall we go?

Wanting to do something
The verb stem in the chart above is also used as the basis of the form that means "want to …", by adding *-tai* to it. This gives the plain form *ikitai* (I) want to go, *tabetai* (I) want to eat. To make this polite, simply add *desu*: *ikitai desu*, *tabetai desu*.

Having to do something
There are several variations on grammatical forms to express this idea, but one will be enough for you. Replace the plain present negative verb ending *-nai* with *nakereba naranai* (plain) or *nakereba narimasen* (polite)

> *ikanakereba naranai* I must/have to go
> *matanakereba narimasen* I must/have to wait

Particles
Particles indicate the grammatical relationships between different parts of the sentence. Some are similar to prepositions in English (to, in, at, from etc), but they follow the noun they refer to; for example, *kyôto kara* "from Kyoto". Others come at the end of a sentence or phrase to change it from a statement to a question, to indicate a contrast or a reason, to add emphasis, and so on.

Particle	Function	Examples
ga	• Marks subject (who or what performs or is described by the verb)	*nihonjin ga san nin imasu* there are three Japanese people
	• Used with certain verbs and *na* adjectives that function like English verbs	*wakaru* understand, *iru* need, *mieru* be visible, *kikoeru* be audible, *suki da* like, *kirai da* dislike
	• Used with potential verb form	*nihongo ga hanasemasu* I can speak Japanese

o	• Marks direct object (who or what the verb is acting upon)	*kudamono o kaimasu* I buy fruit
	• Used with certain intransitive verbs indicating movement	*deru* leave/go/come out, *daigaku o sotsugyô suru* graduate from university, *tai-in suru* leave hospital, *michi o aruku* walk along a path
wa	• Indicates topic of phrase or sentence (who or what the sentence is about)	*watashi wa igirisujin desu* (as for me) I am British
	• Often replaces particles *ga* or *o* to make subject or object into topic of sentence	*sashimi wa tabemasu* as for raw fish, I do eat it (but I'm not commenting on other things I may or may not eat)
	• Can follow particles *ni, de, to* or *e*	*kyôto ni wa ikimasu* I'm going to Kyoto (but not necessarily to other places)
	• Indicates contrast	*tôfu wa tabemasu ga, sashimi wa dame desu* I eat tofu but I don't like/eat raw fish
to	• <u>noun 1</u> *to* <u>noun 2</u> "x and y"	*doyôbi to nichiyôbi* Saturday and Sunday
	• Used in comparisons	*... wa ... to onaji da ...* is the same as ...; *... wa ... to chigau* to be different from ...; *... wa ... to nite iru* to resemble ...
mo	• Indicates addition (also, too, as well); replaces particles *ga, o, wa* or *to*	*jon san mo igirisujin desu* John is British too *kêki mo tabemashita* I ate cake as well (as something else)
	• Can follow particles *ni, de* or *e*	*hokkaidô ni mo ikimasu* I will go to Hokkaidô too

		• "both" <u>noun 1 mo noun 2 mo</u>: "both x and y"; more emphatic than *to*	*supagettî mo piza mo chûmon shita* I have ordered (both) spaghetti **and** pizza
		• <u>interrogative pronoun (eg what, who, where) + mo + negative</u> (nothing, no one, nowhere, etc)	*dare mo imasen* no one is there *nani mo arimasen* nothing is there/I have nothing
ya		• Used to list nouns in a non-exhaustive way	*sakkâ ya tenisu o shimasu* I play football and tennis (among other things)
ka		• <u>noun x ka noun y</u> "or"	*kôhî ka kôcha* coffee or tea
		• <u>interrogative pronoun (eg what, who, where) + ka</u> (something, someone, somewhere, etc)	*dare ka imasu ka?* is anyone there? *doko ka ikimasu ka?* are you going somewhere?
no		• Indicates possession	*tanaka san no hon* Mr/Ms Tanaka's book
		• Indicates that the second noun is described in some way by the first	*onna no hito* woman (literally "female person"); *nihonjin no tomodachi* Japanese friend
		• Replaces noun (one, ones)	*kuroi sêtâ* the black sweater; *kuroi no* the black one
e		• Indicates movement towards	*kyôto e ikimasu* I (will) go to Kyoto
ni		• Indicates destination or goal	*kyôto ni ikimasu* I (will) go to Kyoto
		• Indicates location	*tôkyô ni imasu* I am in Tokyo
		• Indicates a point in time	*shichi ji ni okimasu* I get up at 7 o'clock
		• Marks an indirect object	*tomodachi ni pen o karimashita* I lent my friend a pen

GRAMMAR

de	• Indicates place where an action takes place (in, at, on, etc)	*kyôto de kaimashita* I bought it in Kyoto *uchi de hon o yomimashita* I read a book at home
	• Indicates means by which action of verb is performed	*densha de ikimashita* I went by train *pen de kakimashita* I wrote with a pen
kara	• Indicates a starting point in space (from)	*kyôto kara ikimashita* I went from Kyoto
	• Indicates a starting point in time (from, since)	*san ji kara uchi ni imasu* I will be at home from 3 o'clock *kyonen kara nihonongo o benkyô shite imasu* I have been studying Japanese since last year
made	• Indicates an end point in space (as far as, (up) to)	*kyûshu made ikimasu* I will go to/as far as Kyushu
	• Indicates an end point in time (until)	*jû ji made nemashita* I slept until 10 o'clock

Particles that occur at the end of sentences or clauses

Particle	Function	Examples
ka	• Changes a statement into a question; note that sentence order does not change in any other way	*ashita ikimasu ka?* are you going tomorrow?
ne	• Asks for confirmation or agreement	*ashita ikimasu ne?* you're going tomorrow, aren't you?
yo	• Adds emphasis	*ashita ikimasu yo* I **am** going tomorrow!

to	• Marks a quotation of some kind; used with verbs of saying and thinking; note that the verb it follows must be in the plain form	*tanaka san wa ashita iku to îimashita* Mr/Ms Tanaka said (that) he/she will go tomorrow; *furui to omoimasu* I think (that) it's old
ga	• Indicates contrast (but)	*tenisu wa shimasu ga, sakkâ wa shimasen* I play tennis, but not football
	• Links sentences in a non-contrastive way (sometimes equivalent to "and")	*êga o mi ni ikimasu ga, issho ni ikimasen ka?* I'm going to see a film; would you like to come with me?
kedo (more formally keredomo)	• Indicates contrast (although)	*takai kedo kaimasu* although it's expensive, I'll buy it
kara	• Indicates a reason or cause (so, since, because); note that it always comes at the end of the clause expressing the reason	*byôki da kara, ikimasen* since I'm ill, I won't go/I won't go, because I'm ill; *kono hon wa omoshiroi kara, yonde kudasai* this book is interesting, so please read it
node	• Indicates a reason or cause (so, since, because, given that); note that it always comes at the end of the clause expressing the reason. It is more objective than *kara*.	*kono hoteru wa takai node, tomarimasen* this hotel is expensive, so I won't stay here/I won't stay in this hotel, because it's expensive

Adjectives

There are two kinds of adjectives. One kind, which ends in *i* in the present tense, changes its endings like a verb; the final *i* is replaced by other endings. The other, known as a *na* adjective, is more like a noun. It is followed by some form of the copula; *na* is a special form of *da* used only before nouns.

Some English verbs are *na* adjectives in Japanese: *suki* (to like); *kirai* (to dislike), *jôzu* (to be good at), *heta* (to be bad at). The English verb "to want" is an *i* adjective in Japanese: *hoshî*.

			Affirmative	Negative
Plain form	Present/ future	-i adjectives	nagai (long)	Change i ending to kunai nagakunai
		na adjectives	shizuka da (it is quiet) shizuka na tokoro (a quiet place)	Change da to ja nai shizuka ja nai
	Past	-i adjectives	Change i ending to katta nagakatta	Change kunai ending to kunakatta nagakunakatta
		na adjectives	shizuka datta	shizuka ja nakatta
Polite form	Present/ future	-i adjectives	nagai desu	nagakunai desu
		na adjectives	shizuka desu	shizuka ja arimasen
	Past	-i adjectives	nagakatta desu	nagakunakatta desu
		na adjectives	shizuka deshita	shizuka ja arimasen deshita

Adverbs

Adjectives need to be changed to adverbs to link them to verbs.

i adjective	Change i ending to ku	nagaku tomarimasu stay for a long time; hayaku kaerimasu I'm going home early
na adjective	Change na to ni	kirê ni kaite kudasai please write neatly; jon san wa hashi o jôzu ni tsukaimasu John uses chopsticks skilfully

Interrogative pronouns (question words)

who	*dare* or *donata* (polite)
what	*nan/nani*
when	*itsu*
where	*doko*
how	*dô*
which one	*dore*
which direction/which one (of two)/ where (polite)	*dochira*
what kind of	*donna*

HOLIDAYS AND FESTIVALS

PUBLIC HOLIDAYS

Most of the public holidays (祝日 *shukujitsu*) in Japan centre on "Golden Week", which lasts from the end of April through to the beginning of May. If you plan to travel during this period, be warned that it will be incredibly crowded everywhere, and you will need to book accommodation months in advance and be prepared for steep price increases.

1 January	元日 *ganjitsu* New Year
2nd Monday in January	成人の日 *sêjin no hi* Coming of Age Day
11 February	建国記念の日 *kenkoku kinen no hi* National Foundation Day (anniversary of the founding of the state of Japan by the Emperor Jimmu)
20 or 21 March	春分の日 *shumbun no hi* Spring/Vernal Equinox
29 April	昭和の日 *shôwa no hi* Showa Day (commemorating Emperor Hirohito; known as *midori no hi* Greenery/Nature Day before 2007)
3 May	憲法記念日 *kempô kinen hi* Constitution Day (commemoration of the 1947 Constitution)
4 May	みどりの日 *midori no hi* Greenery/Nature Day (changed from Citizens' Day as of 2007)
5 May	こどもの日 *kodomo no hi* Children's Day
3rd Monday in July	海の日 *umi no hi* Marine Day
3rd Monday in September	敬老の日 *kêrô no hi* Respect for the Aged day
23 September	秋分の日 *shûbun no hi* Autumn Equinox (until 2011)
2nd Monday in October	体育の日 *tai-iku no hi* Health and Sports Day
3 November	文化の日 *bunka no hi* Culture Day
23 November	勤労感謝の日 *kinrô kansha no hi* Labour Day
23 December	天皇誕生日 *tennô tanjôbi* Emperor's birthday

FESTIVALS

Here are just a few of the many Japanese festivals:

New Year celebrations (お正月 *oshôgatsu*): these last three days, from 1 to 3 January. The whole country is on holiday at this time.

Coming-of-age celebration (成人式 *sêjin shiki*): for those reaching 20 years of age this year. Young girls dress up in their best kimonos, and young men in smart suits, and a meal of rice and red beans is prepared and eaten in their honour.

Coming of spring (節分 *setsubun*): held on 3 or 4 February, the beginning of spring in the old lunar calendar. *Setsubun* ceremonies are held to drive away demons and evil spirits: soya beans are thrown into every corner of the house and people shout *oni wa soto! fuku wa uchi!* (Out with demons! In with good fortune!).

Doll's Festival/Girls' day (ひな祭り *hina matsuri*): 3 March. Families set up a seven-tiered stand covered with a red cloth, and place dolls made of porcelain, cloth or paper and representing the imperial household on the tiers. The emperor and empress go at the top, with their servants on the lower tiers. Sweets are given out to children.

Children's day (こどもの日 *kodomo no hi*): held on 5 May, this was traditionally a festival for boys. Miniature samurai helmets are displayed on silk cushions and giant, multicoloured carp streamers (*koinobori*) are hung on poles. The fish are of different sizes to represent all the members of the family.

Star festival (七夕 *tanabata*): celebrated on 7 July or 7 August in different areas. Once a year the paths of the stars Vega and Altair, which symbolize a mythical couple, cross as they pass through the Milky Way. People celebrate by decorating the streets with garlands, and in some cities there are parades of floats decorated with streamers and shooting stars.

Buddhist festival of the dead (お盆 *obon*): 13–15 July. Japanese Buddhists believe that the souls of their ancestors come back to visit them once a year, and they prepare to welcome them when they return. People usually go back to their family homes for this festival.

7-5-3 festival (七五三 *shichi-go-san*) around November 15, children aged three, five and seven are dressed in kimonos and other traditional Japanese costumes and taken to Shintô shrines to pray for good health and long, prosperous lives.

If you get the chance, make sure you see the **cherry blossom** (桜 *sakura*) in April, and the **turning leaves** (紅葉 *kôyô*) in autumn; cherry blossom viewing (花見 *hana mi*) and autumn leaf viewing (紅葉狩り *momijigari*) provide the opportunity for numerous picnics and walks.

USEFUL ADDRESSES

Website of the **Japan National Tourist Organization**: http://www.jnto.go.jp/

IN THE UK

Embassy of Japan, London
101-104 Piccadilly, London W1J 7JT
Tel: 020 7465 6500
Fax: 020 7491 9348

Japan Information and Cultural Centre
(within Embassy of Japan)
Tel: 020 7465 6543/6544
Fax: 020 7491 9347
E-mail: info@jpembassy.org.uk
Website: http://www.uk.emb-japan.go.jp

Consulate General (Visa Section)
Tel: 020 7465 6565
Fax: 020 7491 9328

Consulate General of Japan in Edinburgh
2 Melville Crescent
Edinburgh
EH3 7HW
Tel: 0131 225 4777
Fax: 0131 225 4828

Visa Section
Tel: 0131 225 4777
E-mail: visa.cgj@btconnect.com
Website: http://www.edinburgh.uk.emb-japan.go.jp/index.html

IN THE US

Embassy of Japan, Washington DC
2520 Massachusetts Ave, NW, Washington DC 20008

Tel: 202 238 6700

Fax: 202 328 2187

Website: http://www.us.emb-japan.go.jp/english/html/index.htm

Japan Information and Culture Center
Lafayette Center III
1155 21st Street, NW
Washington, DC 20036-3308
Tel: 202 238 6949
Fax: 202 822 6524
E-mail: jicc@embjapan.org
Website: http://www.us.emb-japan.go.jp/jicc/loc.htm

IN JAPAN

British Embassy, Tokyo
No 1 Ichiban-chô, Chiyoda-ku, Tokyo 102-8381
Tel: (03) 5211-1100
Fax: (03) 5275-3164   (03) 5275 0346 (Consular Section)
E-mail: consular.tokyo@fco.gov.uk (Consular Section)
Website: http://www.uknow.or.jp/be_e/

British Consulate-General, Osaka
Epson Osaka Building, 19F, 3-5-1 Bakuro-machi, Chûo-ku, Osaka 541–0059
Tel: (06) 6120 5600
Fax: (06) 6281 1731
E-mail: bcgosaka@fco.gov.uk

Embassy of the United States, Tokyo
1-10-5 Akasaka, Minato-ku, Tokyo 107-8420
Tel: (03) 3224-5000
Fax: (03) 3505-1862
Website: http://japan.usembassy.gov/t-main.html

US Consulate-General, Osaka-Kobe
Kansai American Center, 2-11-5 Nishitenma, Kita-ku, Osaka 530-8543
Tel: (06) 6315-5965
Website: http://osaka.usconsulate.gov/wwwhmain.html